T0208973

THE EXCHANGE

God's Quid Pro Quo

WAYNE KNIFFEN

WESTBOW
PRESS®
A DIVISION OF THOMAS NELSON
& ZONDERVAN

WestBow Press books may be ordered through booksellers or by contacting:

WestBow Press
A Division of Thomas Nelson & Zondervan
1663 Liberty Drive
Bloomington, IN 47403
www.westbowpress.com
844-714-3454

Scripture taken from the New King James Version® Copyright © 1982 by Thomas Nelson. Used by permission. All rights reserved.

ISBN: 978-1-6642-3730-8 (sc)
ISBN: 978-1-6642-3731-5 (hc)
ISBN: 978-1-6642-3732-2 (e)

Library of Congress Control Number: 2021911935

Print information available on the last page.

WestBow Press rev. date: 6/28/2021

In loving memory of Melanie Jane and Justin Chase Kniffen,
December 6, 1971—January 15, 1997.

Both have made the exchange from the earthly realm
to the heavenly realm (1 Thessalonians 4:13–18).

The noblest thing one can do is to die and go to heaven,
and take someone with you. Melanie did just that.
—Dr. Kenny Digby

CONTENTS

FOREWORD

Before the exploits of some of our elected officials who sold themselves out for personal gain in countries like the Ukraine and China, I am embarrassed to say I did not know what the Latin words *quid pro quo* (this for that) meant. This is ironic considering my Housa interpreter in Jalingo, Nigeria, several years ago translated the exchanged life as *Mu-sain-yah*, meaning, as you might guess, "this for that." I had a basic understanding of God's great exchange through the teaching of Wayne Kniffen and Dorman Duggan in Hereford, Texas, which came from sitting under their teaching for about ten years to date. This book, however, was like years of meetings and revelations rolled up into one moment in time. It was a book I couldn't put down despite having heard the message delivered over time.

This is the point where I tell you that *The Exchange: God's Quid Pro Quo*, like so many other books with flowery forewords written by honored individuals over the years, is truth that will bring change to your life. Well, technically, it won't bring change, but it will bring revelation as to the exchange that Jesus has and will bring to anyone with a desire to know. The difference between change and exchange is important and worth reading about. The concept of exchange is not necessarily new, as there are several fathers in the faith, including Hudson Taylor, nineteenth-century missionary to China, who wrote briefly about it.

Over the years, through the many movements of God in our world, something new and exciting has been revealed by the Holy Spirit of Jesus that brings utter transformation to the body of Christ. It has been five hundred years since the Reformation, but the truth about the exchanged life is just as crucial in our time as the knowledge of the righteous shall live by faith was to the people of Martin Luther's generation, and preceding him, John Wycliffe's. This revelation of what happened to Christ is life-giving and as exciting as the Azusa street revival was in the early days of the twentieth century.

It is truly remarkable how the Holy Spirit can take such a gifted intellectual and give him the ability to communicate complex spiritual truths in ways that all of us can understand. Wayne Kniffen has sprinkled examples and metaphors of spiritual truths about identity and the exchanged life, like the Lord Jesus does Himself. How is that possible? Because, as he states in the book, "Jesus wants to live His life through us, as us." When we begin to grasp who we are in Christ, which should be easily done while reading this book, if we will allow our spiritual senses to drink of the truth that is recorded here, then there will be the fulfillment of the heart of God for all of us: Christ in us, the hope of glory. The exchanged life is Jesus expressing Himself in and through us for the will and purposes of God. Jesus was made what I was (a sinner) so I can be what He is, righteous (2 Corinthians 5:21 NKJV).

I will close with this quote from the book so you can begin reading for yourself:

> Since the transformation—exchange—of a soul is a miracle, it can neither be seen with the physical eye nor understood by the natural mind. That's why it's called a miracle. It's not explicable by natural or scientific laws. The results of a miracle can be observed. What happened to an individual when they accepted Christ as their Lord and Savior will manifest

through their lifestyle. Even though it took place in the invisible realm, it will manifest in the visible realm. This is the purpose of receiving a revelation. It was given to bring about a transformation that leads ultimately to a manifestation, a walking out of what's been worked in.

That is why we need to understand and read *The Exchange: God's Quid Pro Quo*.

David M. Timm, MD, PharmD

INTRODUCTION

Something for something: Our lives for His life.
This for that. Old nature for a new nature.

There's No Such Thing as a Fruitful Telephone Pole

What would you think if you passed by my house and saw me watering the telephone pole that is next to my driveway? You would probably think, *Surely he isn't doing what it looks like he is doing.* The next day you drive by my house again on your way to work, and I'm doing the same thing, I'm watering the telephone pole. This goes on for a week or so. Every day when you pass by, I'm in the front yard, watering the pole.

Finally, your curiosity gets the best of you. On your next drive by, you stop and ask me what I'm doing. When I tell you that I'm watering the telephone pole, you ask a logical question: Why? What would you think if I gave you this ludicrous answer? "I want this pole to produce some fruit, so I'm going to water it until it does." I know what you're thinking: *You can water that pole until the Dallas Cowboys win another Super Bowl if you have a mind to, but it's never going to produce any fruit. It's a telephone pole for crying out loud.*

It's a sheer waste of time, energy, and resources to try to motivate something to do what it doesn't have the ability to do. No matter how much fertilizer and water you saturate a telephone pole with, it will never produce fruit. If fruit is what you're looking for, then you need to exchange the telephone pole for something that has the nature to produce fruit. A telephone pole is a dead tree, and it's incapable of producing anything.

I personally don't know any telephone pole waterers. I probably wouldn't fess up to it if I did. What would that say about me? I've met an inordinate number of people who believe they can impress God and win His acceptance and approval if they do enough good things. We believe that if we can just tip the scales more to our good side, then we might have a shot at winning God's favor. This mindset is deeply rooted in the flesh of every culture.

Being in good standing with God is not about what we can do for Him; it's about what He's already done for us. A person without Christ is like a telephone pole. Religion will have you expend an incalculable amount of time, energy, and resources trying to produce something that God will accept. We water and fertilize our old natures with all kinds of good works. We even learn how to speak Christianese. When it's all said and done, all we have is a well-dressed, attractive telephone pole. It may look good on the outside, but it's still a pole on the inside.

You do know that I'm not talking about telephone poles, right? I'm talking about the apple of God's eye—people. There's a God vacuum residing in every person who longs for acceptance and purpose. Intuitively, individuals know that something is missing in their lives. They may never discover that only God can fill that special spot, but it will be filled by something.

God's Not into Renovation: He's All about Creation

God is not in to renovation, taking something that's old, rundown, and bringing it up to date. He is not in to bringing anything up to code. God is in to creation, bringing something into existence that's never existed before. God is in to new. His mercies are fresh and new every morning (Lamentations 3:22 NKJV).

When a person accepts Jesus as their Lord and Savior, they become a completely new creation. "Therefore, if anyone is in *Christ, he is a new creation*; old things have passed away; behold, *all things have become new*" (2 Corinthians 5:17 NKJV; emphasis added). The word "creation" in this verse goes all the way back to Genesis 1: "In the beginning God *created* (Genesis 1:1 NKJV; emphasis added). To create means to bring something into existence that's never existed before. An individual who says yes to Jesus, becomes a new creation, one that's never existed before. This new person has a new life. The new life they've been given by God is not their old life brought up to code. God is not in to renovation; He is all about creation. A person who's had a born-from-above experience with Christ has been given a brand-new life.

An exchange takes place the moment a person accepts Jesus's invitation to life: God's quid pro quo. Something for something: I give Him me; in return I get Him. This for that: I give Him my old life, He gives me a new life. This is what it means to be born from above, to be a child of God. God didn't renovate the old you. You are a brand-new creation.

No Longer a Worm

The transformation of a worm into a butterfly is intriguing to me. It is a beautiful analogy of what happens to an individual who accepts and receives Jesus Christ as Lord and Savior. A spiritual metamorphosis takes place; something becomes another.

Once a caterpillar enters the cocoon it's made, a transformation takes place on the inside that cannot be seen by the human eye. The worm that went into the cocoon is not what comes out. A butterfly emerges. The transformation that took place on the inside the cocoon is manifested on the outside of the cocoon. The identity of the worm was exchanged for the identity of a butterfly. The worm has gone from being one thing to being something completely different. Once this transformation has taken place, our attention is on what it is—a butterfly—not on the worm it was. The worm has been exchanged for a butterfly, which is nature's quid pro quo.

When a person has a born-from-above experience with Christ, a spiritual transformation takes place. The person's old nature is exchanged for a new nature. Something happens on the inside of a person that cannot be seen by the physical eye. If there's been a spiritual transformation, there will be a physical manifestation of it. What happened on the inside of a person will begin to manifest through their character and conduct.

The reason the majority of believers can't enjoy their new creation lives is because they are still focused on the worm they used to be, their old natures. It's time we begin to enjoy the butterfly we've become, our new creation. I pray this book, *The Exchange: God's Quid Pro Quo*, will help open your understanding to your new identity as a child of God.

1

CHANGE OR EXCHANGE

Think back to that special moment when you became a child of God. When you had your born-from-above experience, were you *changed*, or were you *exchanged*? Does it really matter if we know as long as we're believers? That's a fair question. To know doesn't make you more of a child of God, just as to not know doesn't make you less of a child of God. What it will do is give you a deeper understanding as to who Christ has made you to be.

I have a wonderful friend named Dorman. He's one of those once-in-a-lifetime friends everyone hopes to have someday, the kind of friend who will love you to a fault. In one of our Tuesday pastors' meetings (held at his church for over thirty-five years), I was sharing the biblical definitions of reconciliation, change, and exchange. Even though there are slight nuances of differences in these words, they basically mean the same thing. It's OK to use the word "change" or the word "exchange" when describing your salvation experience. Of the two words, "exchange" will give you a broader view of and a deeper appreciation for your identity in Christ. The exchange that God made for you in the person of Christ was done once, and it's forever.

It's important to understand that the Bible was not written in English. Nor was it written by an American or by someone from Western civilization. Our tendency is to view the scriptures through the eyes of our particular cultural heritage. Sometimes our perception of a particular word may not give us the import of its true meaning. This is what my pastor-friend Dorman said about the word "change": "Our perception of the word 'change' may limit our understanding of what happened to us when we were saved." I think my friend is spot on.

Will there be a change in people after they accept Christ as their personal Savior? Absolutely. This change is the fruit of the exchange. Think about it this way, exchange is the root, and change is the fruit. No exchange, no lasting change. "God was in Christ *reconciling* the world to Himself, not imputing their trespasses to them, and has committed to us the word of *reconciliation*" (2 Corinthians 5:19 NKJV; emphasis added). Paul uses the verb "reconciling" in describing what God did in Christ for us. He uses the noun "reconciliation" to describe what we received. Christ was God in the flesh, exchanging His life for ours, so we could be in right standing with Him.

The Greek word for reconcile is *katallasso*. It means "to exchange," like in exchanging currency. One of the first things you do when you travel to another country is exchange your currency for their currency. You do this so you can access the goods, services, and privileges that particular country has to offer. You could say the exchange of currency is necessary for your survival. We will go into further detail about the reason for the exchange in the next chapter.

Change Can Be Like a Chameleon

Our perception of the word "change" carries with it the idea of moving from one thing to another. We change socks, jobs, opinions, friendships, marriage partners, cars, clothes, churches, ad infinitum. This is our perception of the word "change" in our culture. If this is our understanding of the word "change," then our new birth experience will only be seen and understood from the natural realm. Our Christian experience will be erratic at best. In truth, our identities as believers are established in the spiritual realm.

If we use the word "change" from a Western perspective in trying to understand our identities as a child of God, our focus will be on what we must do for God, not what He's done for us. Understanding change in this light carries with it the idea of something that must be repeated. How many times have you heard a Christian friend say, "I've got to change my ways"? Maybe you've said or thought the same thing. I think it's safe to say most of us have. This is usually said when our walkie-walkie is not matching our talkie-talkie. We're like a chameleon, constantly changing. It all depends on how we're performing.

"You can't go back and change the beginning, but you can start where you are and change the ending" (C. S. Lewis). This may be one of my favorite quotes. It's in the top ten for sure. "You can't go back and change the beginning." Change can do a lot of things, but it can't do anything about the past. The past is what the enemy uses to steal the joy of one's present and the hope of one's future.

It's Time to Reboot Our Spiritual Computers

Change can mean to make or become different. If this was the only way we defined the word "change," then I would say to go with it. The word "exchange" may be a better word to use when describing our coming to Jesus moment. This is the word Paul used when he wrote to the wild church in Corinth to explain what God did to place them in His forever family. What God did, He did one time. It will never need repeating.

Anyone who knows me knows I'm a computer whiz. Not! When I see a computer, I get that deer-in-the-headlights look. Do I run, or do I just stand and stare? I don't know why, but computers intimidate me. That's weird because I use a computer every day. There's so much about computers I don't understand, but there's one thing I do know; when I purchased my computer, it belonged to me. When the credit card machine said, "Accepted," it was mine. I was holding my breath. Everything my computer is capable of doing, all the benefits it can provide, are mine. Here's the catch. If I don't know what it can do or what it contains, I can't access it. Therefore, I can't fully enjoy what's mine because I don't know what's mine. I'm only enjoying a scintilla of the benefits that are available to me.

When you accepted Christ, you got the whole computer. You got it all. Nothing was held back. God didn't save you on an installment plan; you'll get a little here and a little there. What you get is really based on your performance. No. All the birthright privileges of being a child of God belong to you the moment you say yes. But if you don't know what you have in Christ, how can you access and appropriate it. This is why most of us are not living up to our callings. Even though Colossians 2:10 says that we are complete in Christ, most of us are living in spiritual deficit.

If There's no Beginning, There Can Be no Past

The exchange did what change could not do: It took care of your past. The old you was exchanged for a new you, and the new you has no past. The old you had an ending. The new you had no beginning. Are you beginning to see why it's important for us to understand that one's salvation is about exchange and not change?

In the sixth chapter of John's gospel (NKJV), Jesus uses two words to describe the life He and He alone can give to a person who believes in Him. In verse 47 Jesus says the life He gives is "everlasting." Then in verse 54 He says the life He imparts to believers is "eternal." Which is it? Is this new life that's been given to us everlasting or eternal? Your new life in Christ is both everlasting and eternal. These two words come from the same Greek word. This is why you will find them used interchangeably.

The apostle Peter says that Christians are partakers of the Lord's divine nature (2 Peter 1:4 NKJV). In 1 John, believers are described this way: "*as He* (Jesus) *is so are we in this world*" (1 John 4:17 NKJV; emphasis added). The better you know Jesus, the better you'll understand who He's made you to be. What's one of the most staggering attributes that God possess? He's eternal. Eternal means lasting or existing forever, without end or beginning. Now you see why everlasting and eternal are interchangeable. Let me get you to focus on these two words for a moment. Since you share His divine nature and as He is, so are you in this world. Your new life is forever, without end or beginning. It's not easy, but we can wrap our minds around the idea of a life that never ends, but a life that has no beginning, that's in another orbit. Think about this: Who made God? Since God has always been, He has no beginning. Since He has no beginning, He has no past. When you said yes to Jesus, He took your old life and exchanged it for a completely new life that not only has no end, your new life has no beginning. Since your new life has no beginning, the new you, has no past.

Dead Men Don't Eat

You haven't always been a new you. If I were a betting man, I would wager the old you did some things the new you has to deal with today. Decisions have consequences. This is the ammunition the enemy uses to rob us of our identities. He lives up to his job description given in the Gospel of John: "*he comes to steal* and to kill *and to destroy*" (John 10:10 NKJV; emphasis added). The enemy loves to remind you of the bad choices you made before you were saved. Here's the good news. The new you can deal with the consequences of the choices the old you made in the light of who you are now, not who you were then. The new you can also take steps of stupidity that have consequences.

These unwise choices do not contravene who Christ has made you to be. Even though that's true, it doesn't mean we won't have to pay the piper for bad judgment. Payday is not every Friday, but there will be a payday.

"Knowing this, that our old man was crucified with Him, that the *body of evidence might be_done away* with, that we should no longer be slaves to sin" (Romans 6:6 NKJV; emphasis added). Crucifixion was an instrument of death. When Christ was crucified on the cross, our old man was crucified with Him. When Christ died, the old man died. When the old man died, the body of evidence against us was done away with. In a court of law, a case is only as strong as the evidence. If there's no evidence, there's no case. Your old nature was the evidence the enemy had against you. Your old nature was crucified and buried. When that happened, all evidence against you was taken away. The thief wants you to believe the evidence is still alive. Remember, he's a liar and the father of lies.

If we fall for his deception, we'll believe the old man is still alive and well. If that were true, we would have two natures—the old man and the new man—residing in the same house. How in the world do we overpower the old man so the new man can reign? How about this: Let's just feed the new man and starve the old man. If we keep this up long enough, the old man will get weaker, and the new man will get stronger. Sounds logical. But wait a minute. The old man is dead. He was crucified and buried. Dead men don't eat.

If the Old Man Is Dead, Then Who or What Are We Fighting?

I heard a story about a young boxer who was having his first official fight. During the first round, his opponent beat him unmercifully. When he returns to his corner, his trainer tells him, "He hasn't laid a glove on you. In this second round, take it to him." The bell rings, and off the stool he goes, only to be bludgeoned again. Back in his corner, his trainer tells him the same thing, "He hasn't laid a glove on you. Get in there and clean his clock." The third round was a repeat of the first two. Returning to his corner, with both eyes beaten shut, nose flattened, both ears as big as cauliflowers, his trainer gives him the same pep talk. Finally, the young boxer says to his trainer, "I'm going back out there, but you keep your eyes on the referee because somebody out there is beating me like a drum."

Since the old man is dead, then who or what are we fighting? Our battle is with the flesh. What is the flesh? It's our old way of thinking. The flesh is the way we get our needs met independent of God. "Therefore, do not let sin reign in your mortal body, that you should obey it in its lusts. And do not present your members as instruments of unrighteousness to sin, but present yourselves to God as being alive from the dead, and your members as instruments of righteousness to God" (Romans 6:12–13 NKJV). The new you still lives in the same old body. The members of our body have been trained to sin, and they are very good at it. Paul gives us clear instructions on how not to sin. Don't do it (Romans 6:12–13 NKJV)!

Paul told the Galatians, "*Walk in the Spirit*, and you shall not fulfill the *lust of the flesh*" (Galatians 5:16 NKJV; emphasis added). Walking in the Spirit is living life out of your new identity. You're a spiritual being living in a body having a temporary physical experience. The exchange that God made for you in Christ is what took you from the natural realm to the spiritual realm. When we walk in our true identity as children of God, we will not be overcome by a sensual appetite. Nothing on the devil's menu will appeal to us. This is why it's imperative that we know who we are in Christ. I'm not saying that when we know who we are in Christ we will be sinless, but I'm confident we will sin less. God's people are still being defeated because of a lack of knowledge.

A Waste of Time and Effort

If we don't know who we are in Christ, we'll continue to try and change something that doesn't have the capability to change. In the introduction we talked about watering a telephone pole in an attempt to get it to produce fruit. That would be a waste of time, energy, and resources. It doesn't matter how sincere you are either.

This is exactly what we try to do with the old nature. We think that if we expose the old nature to enough church activities, sooner or later it will start producing fruit. We can spend an inordinate amount of time trying to change something that needs to be exchanged.

You may not know this, but that's exactly what happened when you accepted Christ as your Lord and Savior, an exchange took place. You're not the old person made over. When you accepted the Lord's invitation to life, He exchanged you; He exchanged the old you for a new you. You can produce spiritual fruit now because that's your nature.

The more you learn about Jesus, the more you will come to know who you are in Him. Here's a little prayer I encourage you to start praying: "Holy Spirit, show me what I don't know, that I don't know. Show me who I am in Christ." Be ready for an adventure of a lifetime.

2

REASON FOR THE EXCHANGE

A Person without Christ Is Like a Fish Out of Water

I don't think any person with a functioning brain cell would be willing to take a walk in outer space without the proper attire. A space suit provides the environment for a space walker to survive in outer space. Outer space is not the environment humans were created to live in, much less survive in. If an individual chooses to take a stroll in the celestial realm, they must be properly clothed. They must exchange their normal clothing for something that is suitable for surviving in outer space.

A fish out of water can't survive. Water is the environment God created for fish to survive in. A fish dies the moment it's removed from its environment. It may take a few hours before you see the results of its death, but it died the moment it was removed from the water.

A plant removed from the soil is doomed. It dies immediately after being removed from its environment. Like the fish, it may take a little time for its death to be seen, but it died the moment it was removed from the soil.

Like the fish and the plant, Adam became detached from the

environment he was created to survive in. Nobody forcibly removed him. He exercised his free will and stepped out of his environment in willful disobedience. Contrary to popular belief, the soil is not the environment humanity was created to survive in. God formed Adam's dirt suit (body) out of dust from the ground (Genesis 2:7 NKJV). Before God breathed His life into this dirt house, there was no life. The physical body can't know God, can't love God, and can't serve God. It's just an empty house. Without the Spirit of God residing in humanity, there is no life.

God breathed His life into the body, and Adam came alive. God moved in and set up house. The first human became a living soul, a speaking spirit. The environment humankind was created for is God Himself. Outside of God, an individual is like a fish out of water. James says that the body without the Spirit is dead (James 2:26 NKJV).

Now that Adam is full of God, he's acting like God. Adam gives every animal an identity by naming them. Whatever he called them, that's what they became. Adam is acting just like his Creator because he's full of the Spirit of God. He's living in the Spirit, and the Spirit is living in him. "They were both *naked*, the man and his wife, and *were not ashamed*" (Genesis 2:25 NKJV; emphasis added). The word "naked" means exposed. Even though Adam and Eve didn't have clothes on, they were clothed with the glory of God. This is why they were transparent before God and before each other spiritually, emotionally, and physically. When you are in your environment (God) and He's in you, transparency will never be your enemy.

The First Exchange: Life for Death

Chapter 2 of Genesis ends with transparency because Adam is full of God. Chapter 3 ends with a great cover up because Adam is empty of God. An exchange has been made, life for death. Adam exchanged his Spirit-conscious life for a self-conscious life. He moves from Spirit to flesh. He's now getting his needs met independent of God. He's out of his environment. When Adam took the bite of disobedience, he died instantly (Genesis 2:17 NKJV). The manifestation of his death took 930 years (Genesis 5:5 NKJV). The reason it took this length of time is because God's Word will never return void (Isaiah 55:11 NKJV). God told Adam and Eve in Genesis 1, "Be *fruitful and multiply; fill the earth and subdue it*" (Genesis 1:28 NKJV; emphasis added). Humanity's disobedience will never stymie God's plan and purpose.

How did the enemy succeed in getting Adam and Eve to make this exchange? He attacked their identities. The devil is a created being, therefore, he does not have the ability to create. The only thing he can do is counterfeit truth, conceal truth, or contradict truth. He will always attack truth because he is a liar and the father of all lies. There's no truth in him (John 8:44 NKJV).

What tripped Eve's trigger, was when the serpent said, "For God knows that in the day you eat of it your eyes will be open, and *you will be like God*, knowing good and evil" (Genesis 3:5 NKJV; emphasis added). Satan lied to them about their identities. They were already like God. The next thing we hear is the crunching of the fruit. The crunch that was heard around the world. Eve ate fruit from the forbidden tree. Then she gave some to Adam, and he ate. The exchange was made. This was not only a sad day for the first man and woman, it was a sad day for all humankind. Adam and Eve's fall affected us all. Since our seed was in Adam, we were included in the first exchange.

Man's Dilemma

The serpent used the fruit from the forbidden tree as the bait to entice man to bite. It wasn't the bait that cost Adam, it was the bite. The bite was what took him out of his environment. This is exactly how James describes the difference between temptation and sin (James 1:13–15 NKJV). You can use all kinds of bait (temptation) to fish with, but as long as the fish does not bite, it remains safe in its environment. Adam took the bite. Temptation in and of itself is not sin. Jesus was tempted with every temptation that we'll ever face, yet He did not sin. He did not take the bite (Hebrews 4:15; Matthew 4:1–11 NKJV).

There was another tree amid the garden. Adam was free to eat from this tree but chose not to. It's called the tree of life (Genesis 2:9 NKJV). Because of Adam's willful disobedience, God escorted him out of the garden, making the tree of life inaccessible to him (Genesis 3:22 NKJV). God knew that whichever tree Adam chose to eat from, he would bear the nature of that tree. In the very beginning, God made sure that a person did not have two natures, a good one and a bad one. It's very important for us to get hold of this truth. You may want to go back and read the first two chapters of Genesis again.

Here's Adam's dilemma. The tree of life is his only hope for survival, and the way to that tree has been blocked by God (Genesis 3:24 NKJV). Don't forget that the seed of the entire human race was in Adam. His condition is our condition. We didn't inherit Adam's sin, but we did inherit his sinful nature. When we were born, we were born with one nature, and it was sinful. In the New Testament, that old sinful nature is called "'the old man" or the "old self." This is what was exchanged when we had our born-from-above experience (John 3:1–7 NKJV). The old person was exchanged for a new person. The old nature was crucified and buried with Christ (Romans 6:6 NKJV). The new nature was raised with Christ (Romans 6:4 NKJV).

Two trees, two natures. The tree of the knowledge of good and evil was the forbidden tree. God knew what the fruit from that tree would produce. Now Adam knows what God knows about that tree (Genesis 3:22 NKJV). To keep Adam from eating from the tree of life and having two natures, God put him out of the garden. "So He (God) drove out the man (Adam); and He placed cherubim at the east of the garden of Eden, and a flaming sword which turned every way, *to guard the way to the tree of life*" (Genesis 3:24 NKJV; emphasis added). Pay close attention to what God guarded. He guarded the way to the tree of life. Adam no longer had access to the way that led to the tree of life. Let's connect some dots. One day Jesus was talking to His disciples about heaven being a prepared place for prepared people: *"I am the way,* the truth, and the life. No one comes *to the Father* except through Me"* (John 14:6 NKJV; emphasis added). Jesus said, I am the way—without Me there's no going. I am the truth—without Me there's no knowing. I am the life—without Me there's no growing. I think Jesus summed up things pretty well with that statement. Without Him, life is a big fat zero. Hang on to what Jesus said as we make a quick trip back to the garden of Eden.

In Genesis 2, the tree of life was a Christophany. A Christophany is an appearance or nonphysical manifestation of Christ. In Paul's first letter to the Church at Corinth, he recounts the story of Moses and God's people exiting Egypt. He talks about the parting of the sea, and the heavenly manna God provided. He mentions the Rock that life-sustaining water came out of: "All drank the same spiritual drink. For they drank of *that spiritual Rock* that followed them and t*hat Rock was Christ"* (1 Corinthians 10:4 NKJV; emphasis added). That Rock was a Christophany. The Rock was actually a manifestation of Christ in another form.

Now let's flip back to John's gospel and look at what Jesus said about Himself as being the Way. Jesus is literally saying what was closed in the garden of Eden is now open: "I am the way" (John 14:6 NKJV; emphasis added). A way is a path that leads to a place. What was Jesus the way to? The tree of life—Himself: "I am *the way* ... no man comes *to the Father* unless they come through Me" (John 14:6 NKJV; emphasis added). In John 10 Jesus is in the temple being questioned about His identity. His answer almost got Him stoned: "I and My Father are one" (John 10:30 NKJV). When Jesus said that, He was literally saying that He was the only way to the Father. Since Jesus and the Father are one, He's the only way to Himself.

Jesus is the answer to man's dilemma. The environment that man stepped out of in disobedience he now has the opportunity to step back into obedience. God brought to us what we could not return to—Himself.

God Steps Back into Time

When God walked Adam and Eve out of the garden in Genesis 3, God kept walking. He stepped over time and then back into time in Galatians 4. God has the ability to do this because He's not constrained by what He created. God created time. Let's bridge the expanse of time from the Genesis passage to the Galatians passage:

> So He drove out the man; and He placed cherubim at the east of the garden of Eden, and a flaming sword which turned every way, *to guard the way to the tree of life.* (Genesis 3:24 NKJV; emphasis added)

> But *when the fulness of time had come,* God sent forth His Son, born of a woman, born under the law. (Galatians 4:4 NKJV; emphasis added)

By connecting these two verses that are separated by millenniums, we are able to see what God had in mind before there was the beginning of time. The way to the tree of life in the garden of Eden may have been blocked because of Adam's and Eve's disobedience, but God opened the way to Himself by sending His Son wrapped in an earth suit. The exchange was set up, God's quid pro quo. By His grace God brought to humanity what humanity could not return to, the environment for humankind's survival—Himself.

The Way to the Tree of Life becomes Inaccessible

Try to grasp the far-reaching consequences that Adam's and Eve's disobedience to God's Word created. They were removed from the presence of God. In Genesis 3 God walked humanity out of the garden of Eden. The reason Adam and Eve were expelled from the garden was because they did exactly what God told them not to do; they ate the fruit from the tree of the knowledge of good and evil. They now bear the nature of that tree, which is getting their needs met independent of God. To keep them from eating from the tree of life, which would give them two natures, God escorted Adam and Eve from the garden. Then He made the way to the tree of life inaccessible. God stationed mighty angels at the east of the garden, and He placed a flaming sword at the entrance to guard the way to the tree of life. God closed the door to the garden, and when God closes a door, no one can open it (Revelation 3:7–8 NKJV). Humanity is now left to provide for themselves by the sweat of their brow (Genesis 3:17–19 NKJV). That's the fruit from the root of the tree they chose to eat from. It looks like God's experiment with creation was a failure. Don't forget, the seed of the entire human race was in Adam. So the way to the tree of life was not only closed to him but to the entire human race. Adam's fall affected us all.

Was the creation of humanity a colossal failure? When God walked out of the garden with Adam and Eve, I assure you He wasn't wondering what He was going to do now that humanity had failed. Since God is all-knowing, nothing will ever frustrate His plans or foil the works of His hands. Revelation 13 must have been on His mind: "The Lamb (Jesus) Who was *slaughtered before the world was made*" (Revelation 13:8 NLT; emphasis added). When God escorted Adam and Eve out of the garden, He kept walking, stepping over time, until it was time for Him to step into time, when it was the fullness of time (Galatians 4:4). God, who brought all creation into being by the spoken word, now expresses Himself as the living Word through a little baby in a manger:

> In the beginning was the Word, and the Word was with God, and *the Word was God.* He was in the beginning with God. All things were made through Him, and without Him nothing was made that was made. And *the Word became flesh and dwelt among us,* and we beheld His glory, the glory as of the only begotten of the Father, full of grace and truth. (John 1:1–3, 14 NKJV; emphasis added)

One translation says the Word became human.

From Eden to Bethlehem

Let's transition from the garden of Eden to a manger in Bethlehem. What's going on here? God is setting up the exchange. The Word is becoming flesh (John 1:14 NKJV). Jesus Christ was divinity wrapped up in humanity. Jesus was the human side; Christ was the divine side. The human side is what made the God side legal to be on the earth. The God side is what gave the human side the authority to operate here on the earth. By coming to the earth this way, God did not violate His Word. He had given the authority over the earthly realm to humanity (Genesis 1:26–28 NKJV). Since He is a God of His word, He never rescinded that commission.

God used Mary's womb as the vehicle to bring Himself in to the world. Preparation for this was done before Satan ever entered the garden. God took a piece of the first man He created to form the first woman. She was a special design in every way. The woman was created with a womb, giving her the ability to carry a child. The umbilical cord would allow oxygen and nutrients to flow from her body to the baby during the gestation period. God designed it so that the blood of the mother would not mingle with the child's blood. The blood of the child would be determined by the father. Knowing this gives us a better insight into what Isaiah meant when he said, "For unto us *a Child will be born*, Unto us a Son is given" (Isaiah 9:6 NKJV; emphasis added). Mary would be the mother of the Child (Jesus), but the Son (Christ) would be sent: "But when the fullness of time had come, *God sent forth His Son*, born of woman, born under the law" (Galatians 4:4 NKJV; emphasis added). If you've ever wondered why God didn't intervene when Satan was tempting Eve in Genesis 3, now you know; He did intervene! Satan's defeat was a sure thing.

Let me repeat what I have already said. The incarnation was God bringing to humanity what humanity couldn't return to, the environment for its survival—Himself. The way to eternal life was blocked in the garden because of Adam's disobedience. The way to eternal life is now open and available to all who respond to Jesus Christ in obedience. Whosoever will, may come.

The word "Bethlehem" means "house of bread." Keep that in mind as you read what Jesus said about Himself: "I am the bread of life" (John 6:48 NKJV). "*I am the living bread* which came down from heaven. *If anyone eats this bread, he will live forever*; and the bread that I shall give is My flesh, which I shall give for the life of the world" (John 6:51 NKJV; emphasis added). It's no coincidence that the Bread of Life (Jesus) was born in the house of bread.

There's an obvious connection between Jesus, the living bread, and the tree of life that was in the garden. All humanity is faced with the same choice that Adam and Eve had in the garden of Eden, to obey God or not to obey. A person will bear the nature of their choice. Life or death is in the eating. You are what you eat. Choose wisely.

The Exchange of Seed

God set a principle in motion at the very beginning of time that can never be changed: "Seed will bear after its kind" (Genesis 1:11–12

NKJV). If you plant corn seed, don't be surprised when you get corn and not cotton. Identity (DNA) is in the seed. What you harvest is determined by what you plant.

The seed of the entire human race was in the first Adam. After Adam sinned, he bore children after his own image: "When Adam was one-hundred-thirty years old, he became the father of a son who was just like him—in his very image" (Genesis 5:3 NLT). Seed will bear after its own kind. When Adam sinned, his seed became corrupted. This corrupted seed was passed on to all humanity: "Yes, *Adam's one sin brings condemnation for everyone*" (Romans 5:18 NLT; emphasis added). The entire human race inherited Adam's sinful nature.

Thank God for the last Adam, whose seed is incorruptible. "But the last Adam—that is Christ—is a life-giving Spirit" (1 Corinthians 15:45b NLT). "But *Christ's one act of righteousness brings a right relationship with God and new life for everyone*" (Romans 5:8 NLT; emphasis added). There was a seed exchange. The sinful seed (old nature) we inherited from Adam was exchanged for the sinless seed (new nature) of Christ when we had our born-from-above experience. "Just as everyone dies because we belong to Adam, everyone who belongs to Christ will be given new life" (1 Corinthians 15:22 NLT).

When we accepted and received Jesus as our Lord and Savior, there was a seed exchange. The old sinful seed that we inherited from Adam, wasn't cleaned up and made better; it was completely exchanged for the new sinless seed that comes from the last Adam, Christ. As Adam did not bear the nature of both trees in the garden, we do not bear both the sinful seed of Adam and the sinless seed of Christ. It's one or the other, not both. A person is in Christ or in Adam. As a believer, Jesus is our tree of life, he is our living bread.

Everyone has been gifted with a free will. We have the freedom of choice. An individual can choose life, or one can choose death. God will not force our decision. "If you openly declare that Jesus is Lord and believe in your heart that God raised Him from the dead, you will be saved. For it is by believing in your heart that you are made right with God, and it is by openly declaring your faith that you are saved" (Romans 10:8–10 NLT).

When God stepped over time and then back in to time when it was the right time, He was making Himself available, accessible, and approachable to everyone. God did for us what we could not do for ourselves. He came into the world where we are because we could not return to where He is; that door had been closed. God came to us in the person of His Son, Jesus Christ. Jesus said, "*I am the door.* If anyone enters by Me, he will be saved, and will go in and out and find pasture" (John 10:9 NKJV; emphasis added). Jesus is the only door that gives humanity access to God.

"God was in Christ *reconciling* (exchanging) the world to Himself, not imputing their trespasses to them, and has committed to us the word of *reconciliation* (exchange)" (2 Corinthians 5:19 NKJV; emphasis added). Becoming a new creation in Christ is not about change, the old becoming better. It's about exchange, the old becoming *another.* God made this exchange through His Son: "The Scripture tells us, 'The first man, Adam, became a living person.' But the last Adam— that is, Christ—is a life-giving Spirit" (1 Corinthians 15:45 NLT). Something was exchanged for something: God exchanged the old nature for a new nature, and He did it through His Son, Jesus Christ. The exchanged life is God's quid pro quo.

3

EXPERIENCE VS. TRUTH

If we accept the written Word's (Bible) description of the living word (Jesus), then why is it so difficult for us to accept the written Word's description of who we are in Christ? *"As He is, so are we in this world"* (John 4:17 NKJV; emphasis added). The better we know Jesus, the better we will know who we are as new creations (2 Corinthians 5:17 NKJV). To know Him is to know who we are in Him.

Dumbing Down Truth to Match Our Experiences

The majority of believers will say that the Word of God is the plumb bob for what they believe about life. It should be, but the raw truth is it's not true. Our experiences usually determine what we really believe. Pose this question to a Bible class: "Will all the saints and righteous people in class please raise your hands?" You probably will not get many raised hands, if any. Why? Experience. Even though the Word of God addresses believers as saints and declares that we are righteous, we really don't believe it because it doesn't line up with our experiences. We don't feel like saints, and we certainly don't act righteous at times. Our experiences don't match the truth about our identities. Instead of going with the truth (the Word of God), we go with our experiences.

How many times have you heard a child of God say, "I'm just a sinner saved by grace"? That's dumbing down truth to match our experiences. We are saved by grace, and we certainly do sin, but that doesn't make us sinners saved by grace. What we need to do is demand that our experiences rise to the level of truth. Truth never changes, but our experiences do. The truth is, we are saints who sometimes sin.

Before we were recipients of the great exchange, we were sinners by nature. What do sinners do? They sin. Why does a dog bark? Does it bark because it's a dog, or is it a dog because it barks? I think the answer is obvious. A dog barks because its nature is to bark. A barking dog may be annoying, but it's not surprising. Before Christ, we had two problems: who we were and what we did. We were sinners by nature. What do sinners do? They sin because it's their nature to sin. Christ came to take care of both problems, who we were and what we did. He took care of the dog and the bark.

Two Problems, Two Solutions

The blood and the cross took care of these two problems. The blood that Christ spilled took care of our sin problem. "And according to the law almost all things are purified with blood, and *without shedding of blood there is no remission*" (Hebrews 9:22 NKJV; emphasis added). "Whom God set forth as a propitiation *by His blood*, through faith, to demonstrate His righteousness, because in His forbearance God had passed over the sins that were previously committed, to demonstrate at the present time His righteousness, that He might be just and the justifier of the one who has faith in Jesus" (Romans 3:25–26 NKJV; emphasis added). "Much more then, having now been *justified by His blood*, we shall be saved from wrath through Him" (Romans 5:9 NKJV; emphasis added). The blood that Christ shed for our sins did what the blood of an animal could not do. The blood of a sacrificial animal only covered sin. This is why the sacrifice had to be repeated over and over again. The perfect Lamb's (Jesus's) blood removed our sins once and for all time (Hebrews 10:4–14 NKJV).

The blood of Christ took care of the sin, but what about who we were? What about our old, sinful natures? The cross of Christ took care of that too. "Knowing this, that *our old man was crucified with Him*, that the body of sin might be done away with, that we should no longer be slaves of sin" (Romans 6:6 NKJV; emphasis added). "For He (God) made Him (Jesus) *who knew no sin to be sin for us*, that we might become the righteousness of God in Him" (2 Corinthians 5:21 NKJV; emphasis added). Jesus was made what we were, so we could be what He is. Let me say it another way: What we were, Jesus was made (sin), so that what He is, we became (righteous). The cross of Christ took care of our old natures. This is the exchanged life; the sinner was exchanged for a saint. We are new creations with a new nature, God's quid pro quo.

As new creations do we sin? Yes. Is it natural for us as new creations to sin? No. For a saint to sin is like a dog meowing; it goes against its nature. Knowing our identities in Christ will not make us sinless, but it sure will make us sin less. Just because a child of God sins does not make them a sinner saved by grace. It proves they really don't have a healthy understanding of the new creation they have become in Christ. It's an identity crisis.

Sin didn't die; the sinner did. As a child of God, sin is not dead to us. We are dead to sin. Liver is not appealing to me whatsoever, but liver is not dead to me. I'm dead to liver. Liver is not attractive to me. I don't like liver, and I don't like people who do. We still live in a fallen world. What we need to keep in mind is we are *in* the world, but we are not *of* the world. When we get a revelation of our true identities in Christ and His amazing grace, sin will lose its attraction and its appeal.

Becoming a Mature Example of Who We Already Are

When God blessed me with children, my prayer for them was not that they grow up to be human beings. Why wouldn't that be my prayer? Because they were born human beings. My prayer was that they would grow and mature into loving, God-fearing, responsible adults. My desire was for them to become mature examples of who they already were.

That's what sanctification is all about. It's a process of discovering who you already are as a child of God. The understanding that most believers have about sanctification is that it's an act or process of being made righteous and holy. To embrace the truth that we are already righteous and holy is an alien concept to most Christians because of their experiences.

Martin Luther, who began the Protestant Reformation, did the community of faith a big favor when the Word of God became more important to him than the tenets of the established religion of his day. Luther defined salvation this way: "Salvation, eternal life, are not earned by good deeds but are received only as a free gift of God's grace through the believer's faith in Jesus Christ. The bible is the only source of divinely revealed knowledge." Kudos to Mr. Luther. He nailed justification—pun intended—but I'm convinced he was awry on sanctification.

It's OK to think of sanctification as a process—if we understand process. It's not a process of becoming who we will be in Christ. Sanctification is a process of discovering who we already are in Christ. If we make it a process of becoming who we will be in Christ, our emphasis will be on ourselves and what we have to do to achieve righteousness and holiness. If we see sanctification as a process of discovering that Christ has already made us righteous and holy, our emphasis will be on Christ.

Another Protestant reformer, Zacharius Ursinus (1534–1583), wrote, "God grants and credits to me the perfect satisfaction, righteousness, and holiness of Christ, as if I had never sinned nor been a sinner, as if I had been perfectly obedient, as Christ was obedient for me." This man nailed sanctification.

If we accept what the Bible says about Jesus and His identity, why is it so hard for us to accept what the Word of God says about our identity as His children: *"As He is so are we in this world* (1 John 4:17 NKJV; emphasis added). The answer is simple. It's because of our experiences. We do things and say things that we shouldn't do or say, and then we hear that we are sinners saved by grace. That sounds legit because it matches our experiences. So we go with our experiences at the expense of the truth.

Are Our New Identities Positional or Literal?

"For as by *one man's* (Adam) *disobedience* many were *made sinners,* so also by *one Man's* (Jesus) *obedience* many will be *made righteous"* (Romans 5:19 NKJV; emphasis added). The first Adam was disobedient, and he passed on his nature through his seed. The last Adam (Jesus) was obedient, and He passed on His nature through His seed. Before we had our born-from-above experience with Christ, we were in the first Adam. We bore his sinful nature. Were we literal sinners or positional sinners? I'll answer that for you. We were literal sinners because our natures were sinful. Our experiences submit to that truth. We were not positional sinners.

Once the exchange has been made and we are in Christ, we bear His nature (2 Peter 1:4 NKJV). We are not positionally righteous. The old you has been exchanged for a new you. The sinner has been exchanged for a saint. We are literally righteous because we are new creations (2 Corinthians 5:17 NKJV). The old you was not a positional sinner, and the new you is not positionally righteous. The new you is literally righteous and holy. It's time we start living up to our identities.

Some may say, "I don't feel righteous and holy." Feelings can be fickle, and our feelings can lie to us. Feelings are real, but they may not be true. I can feel God doesn't love me, but that isn't the truth. He's madly in love with me. He has given me His word that He will never turn His heart from me (Hebrews 13:5 NKJV). That's true on the days when I have my A game, and it's true on the days when I can't find my game. Feelings are constantly changing where truth is unchangeable. Truth will trump facts every time. This is why Jesus said that if we abide in His Word, we will know the truth, and the truth we know will set us free (John 8:31–32 NKJV). Feelings are not fundamental to faith, so don't allow your feelings to be the thermostat that controls your life.

We deal with facts the same way we deal with feelings. Facts are real, but facts may not be true. As a child of God, we acknowledge facts, but we confess truth. Here's an example. I acknowledge the fact that I'm not feeling well, but I confess I'm healed. To confess means, "to say the same thing"; to say what the Word of God says. I don't feel well; that's my acknowledgment. My confession is, by His stripes I'm healed (Isaiah 53:5 NKJV; 1 Peter 2:24 NKJV). My confession is agreeing with the Word of God. Jesus said the Word of God is truth, not facts or feelings (John 17:17 NKJV). As believers, we acknowledge facts, but we confess truth. Truth will trump facts every time.

Truth That You Know Will Set You Free

As a young boy growing up, I was what you might call mischievous. That's the label I got tagged with. I'd rather say that I was a young man who had been endowed with a lot of energy and had a lot of unharnessed potential. OK, I was a runaway talent. Whenever something happened at school that was outside the perimeters of acceptance, it was my name that was called. It was not uncommon to hear a teacher or principal say something like, "We have a pretty good idea who did this [they would name the infraction], so we would encourage you to go ahead and fess up." Their follow-up statement would be, "The truth will set you free, young man." It might take a while, but I would usually fess up. I will tell you this, coming clean didn't make me free. It usually made me a little sore, but not free. That was back in the day when a good ole spanking was usually the number-one option. A principal or teacher didn't have to have written permission from a parent to administer corporal punishment. If you got a spanking at school, guess what you got when you got home.

The truth will set you free. What is truth? This is basically how the world defines truth. Truth is being in accord with fact or reality; it's fidelity to an original standard. Truth is what's real. A thing is true if it is a fact. The Greek philosopher Aristotle (384 BC–322 BC) gave a shot at defining truth: "To say of what is that it is not, or of what is not that it is, is false, while to say of what is that it is, and of what is not that it is not, is true." You may what to chew on that for a while. Aristotle is so close in his definition of truth, but so far away.

Are feelings real? Absolutely they are, but they may not be true. We confuse something that's real as being true. A person may feel that God doesn't love them. Those feelings are real, but they are not true. God loves you no matter how you feel. Thoughts are real, but are they always true? Just because something is real doesn't mean it's true. If we rely on our feelings and thoughts for judging truth, we are in for a bumpy ride because our thoughts and feelings are constantly changing. Truth is immutable.

What is truth according to the Word of God? Truth is constant and unchangeable. What truth was in the past it is in the present, and it will be in the future. Truth is a quality intrinsic to the very nature of God, and it was fully expressed in His Son, Jesus Christ: "And the Word (Jesus) became flesh and dwelt among us, and we beheld His glory, the glory as of the only begotten of the Father, *full of grace and truth*" (John 1:14 NKJV; emphasis added). Jesus is the complete measure of grace and truth in its limitless extent. "Jesus Christ is the same yesterday, today, and forever" (Hebrews 13:8 NKJV). Truth never changes.

Jesus makes a bold declaration about Himself in John 14: "I am the way, *the truth*, and the life. No one comes to the Father except through Me" (John 14:6 NKJV; emphasis added). Jesus is the ultimate expression of truth. There is no truth apart from Jesus.

What is the point in making a big deal out of this? If we accept the truth about what the scriptures say about Jesus, then why is it so difficult for us as believers to accept what the written Word says about us? I think we're left with only one answer. Many times our experiences do not line up with the Word of God. When that happens, our tendency is to embrace our experiences over the truth. What we're doing unknowingly is dumbing down the truth to match our experiences. If I've sinned, then the truth must be I'm a sinner saved by grace. What we should be doing is demanding that our experiences rise to the level of truth. I'm a saint who sometimes sins.

Jesus never said that truth will set anyone free. What He did say was, "if you will abide in My word, you will know the truth, and the truth you know, will set you free" (John 8:31–32 NKJV). The truth that we become intimate with from abiding in the Word of God is what sets us free. The truth we know from spending time in the Word will also keep us free.

What about reality? When we sin, doesn't that prove that we're sinners saved by God's grace? Our experiences don't determine reality. Reality is whatever God says about something. When we take steps of stupid (sin), it proves we don't understand God's truth about our identities as new creations. Reality is God's view of something, not our experiences.

The Indwelling Presence of the Spirit of Truth

Jesus told His disciples that the day would come when He would return to His Father. They were not to worry because the Father would send them another Helper, who would abide with and in them forever. The word "another" means, "another of the same kind." This Helper who the Father would send to be their permanent companion would be exactly like Jesus—the same kind. Since Jesus said He was the truth, the Holy Spirit had to be the truth as well. "The *Spirit of truth*, whom the world cannot receive, because it neither sees Him nor knows Him, but you know Him, for *He dwells with you and will be in you*" (John 14:17 NKJV; emphasis added). As a believer, a new creation in Christ, you have the Spirit of truth living inside you. He knows everything about everything, and He's promised to teach you all things. "But the Helper, the Holy Spirit, whom the Father will send in My name, He will teach you all things, and bring to your remembrance all things that I said to you" (John 14:26 NKJV).

Whatever the Spirit of truth says about you is reality. You are who He says you are, even when it goes against your thoughts, your feelings, and your experiences. Whatever He says is reality. This is the truth that sets us free.

> And we know (absolute settled knowledge) that the Son of God has come, and He has given us understanding so that we can know the true God. And now we live in fellowship (union) with the true God because we live in fellowship (union) with His Son, Jesus Christ. He is the only true God, and He is eternal life. (1 John 5:20 NLT)

Since we have been given a free will, we have a choice. Do we allow our experiences to determine our identities, or do we allow God's Word to identify us? We can allow our experiences to determine our realities, or we can embrace what the Spirit of truth says is reality. The ball is in our court. Keep this in mind as you consider your options: Truth trumps facts every time. When we begin to allow the truth of God to determine our identities, we will find that our experiences will begin to rise to the level of truth. The more truth we know, the more freedom we will experience. What truth was it still is, and it will always be.

The new life that we have in Christ came from an exchange, not a change. God did not take the old you and renovate it. You're not an updated model of the old you. You are a brand-new creation who has never existed before (2 Corinthians 5:17 NKJV). There's been an exchange of identities. The truth you know will set you free. What truth was in the past, it is in the present, and it will be in the future.

4

TWO REALMS:
THE SEEN AND THE UNSEEN

"By faith we understand that the worlds were framed by the word of God, so that the *things which are seen were not made of things which are visible*" (Hebrews 11:3 NKJV; emphasis added). The things we are *able* to see are not made out of things we *can* see. That leaves us with only one conclusion. The things we are able to see are made out of things we cannot see. OK. That may sound a little sci-fi to most of us. The last part of this verse is so fascinating that we forget what the writer says in the first part of the verse. The entire universe was formed and framed by God's spoken word.

Flashback

This verse takes us back to and connects us with the creation story, how the created physical realm came to be. God steps out of the unseen realm into the seen realm and begins to call things into existence with His spoken word. Things that could not be seen before can now be seen. The order intrigues me. What could not be seen can now be seen. Let that sit on the front burner of your mind for a moment. The unseen realm is more real than the seen realm.

There are two realms—the realm that can't be seen, and the realm that can be seen. Instead of the word "realm," we could use the words "kingdom," "arena," "domain," "sphere," "region," "zone," or "world." Choosing one of these words may help clarify for us what the writer of Hebrews is talking about. The world that we're able to see with our physical eyes came from a realm that we can't see with our physical eyes. To make things even more fascinating, the world we can't see is more real than the world we can see. "While we do not look at the things which are seen, but at the things which are not seen. For the things which are seen are temporary, but the things which are not seen are eternal" (2 Corinthians 4:18 NKJV).

Flash-Forward

After Jesus had been arrested in the garden of Gethsemane and taken before Pilot, He was asked this question, *"Are You the King of the Jews"* (John 18:33 NKJV; emphasis added)? Jesus's answer is worth paying attention to. "My kingdom is *not of this world*. If My kingdom were *of this world*, My servants would fight, so that I should not be delivered to the Jews; but now My kingdom *is not from here*" (John 18:36 NKJV; emphasis added). Sometimes we need to pay attention to what a person doesn't say to hear what they really say. Jesus didn't say His kingdom was not *in* this world, he said His kingdom was not *of* this world. One of the first things Jesus said when He began His public ministry was, "From that time Jesus began to preach and to say, Repent, for *the kingdom of heaven is at hand*" (Matthew 4:17 NKJV; emphasis added). Heaven's government, the rule of God, has arrived in the seen realm. The kingdom of God, in the person of Jesus, was now in the world (in the seen realm), but the kingdom of God is not of the world.

In the Lord's prayer, Jesus prays for His disciples. "I do not pray that You should take them *out of the world*, but that You should keep them from the evil one. They are not *of the world*, just as I am not *of the world*" (John 17:15–16 NKJV; emphasis added). The disciples were in the world, but they were not of the world. Even though I've said this several times, it needs to be repeated because it is so crucial to our understanding the new creation life. There are two realms, two worlds, two kingdoms––the one we can see, the one we can't see. The one that can't be seen by our natural eyes is more real than the one we're able to see with our natural eyes.

Why is it important for us to know there are two realms? So we'll have a better understanding of who we are as new creations and how we use the currency of faith to access the resources available to us in the spiritual realm while living in the physical realm. Even though we're presently living in this neighborhood, our citizenship is in heaven (Philippians 3:20 NKJV).

The Natural and the Spiritual

The Word of God separates people into two categories, the natural and the spiritual. There is no in-between, no third group. The natural person is the individual who has never had a born-from-above experience. "But *the natural man* does not receive the things of the Spirit of God, for they are foolishness to him; nor can he know them, because they are spiritually discerned" (1 Corinthians 2:14 NKJV; emphasis added). This verse says three things about someone who has never made the exchange. The natural person cannot receive anything from the Holy Spirit. They don't have a "spiritual receiver." Second, the things of God are foolish to them. This verse doesn't say the things of God *appear* to be foolish to them, they *are* foolish to them. The third reason is devastating. The natural person can't know the things of God. The things of God are spiritually discerned, and a natural person is spiritually dead.

A person who's in the natural state may know about God but

doesn't know God. They may know about Jesus, but they don't know Jesus. When a natural person's death is manifested, they will never have another opportunity to have a born-from-above experience. There will be an eternal separation from God. A person who's not had a born-from-above experience with Christ, is as worse off as they possibly can be. You can't be any worse off than to be separated from God for all eternity. "For the message of the cross is foolishness to *those who are perishing*, but to us who are being saved it is the power of God" (1 Corinthians 1:18 NKJV; emphasis added). A person who has not accepted the exchange God offers, His life for theirs, is already dead, waiting to die. A natural person is confined to the seen—the physical—realm and has no access to the unseen—spiritual—realm.

"But *he who is spiritual* judges all things, yet he himself is rightly judged by no one" (1 Corinthians 2:15 NKJV; emphasis added). This verse begins with the conjunction of contrast, "but." The spiritual person is totally opposite of the natural person. The spiritual person can and does receive from God. A person who has made the exchange from sinner to saint has the ability to receive from God and process what is received. A spiritual person lives in the seen—physical—realm, but they have access to the unseen—spiritual—realm. The things in the unseen realm are accessed by the currency of faith.

The Big Five

"But solid food belongs to those who are of full age, that is, those who by reason of use have *their senses exercised* to discern both good and evil" (Hebrews 5:14 NKJV; emphasis added). Our physical senses are the faculties of sight, smell, hearing, taste, and touch. Sometimes these are referred to as the "big five." We see with our eyes, we smell with our noses, we listen with our ears, we taste with our tongues, and we touch with our skin. Our sense organs send information to our brains to help us understand and perceive the world around us, the seen realm.

Our five physical senses, which come as standard equipment at birth, enable us to connect and interact with our physical environments. Hebrews 5 is not talking about training the big five. "But solid food belongs to those who are of full age, that is, those who *by reason of use have their senses exercised to_discern both good and evil*" (Hebrews 5:14 NKJV; emphasis added). The writer of Hebrews is talking about having our *spiritual senses* trained, so we can detect and differentiate between good and evil. We are spiritual beings temporarily living in a physical world. Our spiritual senses enable us to connect and interact with our spiritual environments. A person who has not had a born-from-above experience, doesn't have this ability. Why? Because they are spiritually dead (1 Corinthians 1:18 NKJV; Ephesians 2:1, 5 NKJV).

As discussed elsewhere in this book, when God set in motion the beginning of time, He planted two trees in the middle of the garden of Eden (Genesis 2:9 NKJV). Adam was given the freedom to eat from all the trees in the garden, which included the tree of life. There was one exception. He was not to eat from the tree of the knowledge of good and evil (Genesis 2:16–17 NKJV). We know how that went down don't we? Adam disobeyed God when he ate fruit from the forbidden tree. Here's a question we need to ask ourselves: Did God know what would happen if Adam chose to eat from the tree of the knowledge of good and evil? Absolutely He did. After Adam disobeyed God by eating fruit from the forbidden tree, he now knows what God knows about that tree: "Then the Lord God said, 'Behold, the man has become like one of Us, *to know good and evil*. And now, lest he put out his hand and take also of the tree of life, and eat, and live forever.'—Therefore the Lord God sent him out of the garden of Eden" (Genesis 3:22–23 NKJV; emphasis added). God knew that Adam would bear the nature of whichever tree he chose to eat from. To keep him from eating from the tree of life, and bearing two natures, Adam and his covenant partner, Eve, were removed from the garden.

The first exchange was made in the third chapter of Genesis. Adam's disobedience took him from being spirit-conscious, to being self-conscious. He exchanged life for death (Genesis 2:17 NKJV). He's left with only the ability to connect and interact with his physical world that he contaminated with his disobedience through his physical senses, the big five. The purpose of salvation, God's quid pro quo, is to move a person from being self-conscious to being spirit-conscious. The things of God are spiritually discerned, and a natural person is spiritually dead.

A natural person is limited to their physical senses in the natural, seen, realm. A spiritual person has the ability to relate to both the natural seen realm and the spiritual unseen realm. That's what the writer of Hebrews is saying. Our spiritual senses are strengthened when we use them. In other words, by practice.

A Person's Greatest Need

If you were to ask the question, "What is a person's greatest need?" the majority answer would be forgiveness. It's a great answer, but there's only one thing wrong with it. It's not true. Paul gives us the answer to a person's greatest need in the book of Ephesians: "And you *He made alive, who were dead* in trespasses and sins ... even when *we were dead* in trespasses, *made us alive* together with Christ [by grace you have been saved]" (Ephesians 2:1–5 NKJV; emphasis added). Before we were made alive in Christ, we were dead. What does a dead person need? They need life! This is our answer to the question, "What is humanity's greatest need?"

Before we were made alive in Christ, all we could relate to was our physical world, the seen realm, which is passing away (1 John 2:17 NKJV). Now that we've been made alive in Christ, we are in the world, but we're not of the world. This is what the exchange—God's quid pro quo—is all about. We exchange death for life. Forgiveness is a part of this life package as well as all the other birthright benefits that come from being new creations in Christ.

Assumption Is the Lowest Form of Knowledge

The natural person mentioned in 1 Corinthians 2:14 may think that anyone who hears from God is a little weird or even foolish. Since they don't hear God speak, they assume no one else does either. Assumption is the lowest form of knowledge. Beautiful music is not beautiful to someone who does not have the ability to hear. A gorgeous sunset is not gorgeous to someone who can't see. The incredible aroma of smoking barbecue doesn't smell good to someone who can't smell. We must be in possession of physical senses before we can connect and interact with our physical environments. In like manner, it takes a born-from-above experience to be in possession of spiritual senses. Our spiritual senses are what make it possible for us to connect and interact with our spiritual environments.

As a child of God, we are spiritual beings living in a physical world. We have physical senses that enable us to connect and interact with our physical realms. We also have spiritual senses that empower us to connect and interact with the spiritual realm. We are spirit beings who have souls, and we live in bodies.

The Unseen Can Be Seen through the Eyes of Faith

There's a great story in 2 Kings 6 that may provide us with a better understanding of the coexistence of the natural realm and the spiritual realm, the seen and the unseen. The king of Syria was making war against Israel. The king called in his officers and gave them the battle plan. He told them to mobilize all their forces at a certain place. They were to set up camp and prepare to ambush the army of Israel. There was something very important that the king did not consider when he made his battle plans against Israel. Heaven had a spy in the land. His name was Elisha. Every time the king tried to set his trap, Elisha would inform the king of Israel. This happened time and time again. Finally, the king of Syria became very upset and called his officers in for a meeting. He demanded to know who the traitor was among them. One of the officers spoke up and said, "It's not us, my lord the king. Elisha, the prophet in Israel, tells the king of Israel even the words you speak in the privacy of your bedroom" (2 Kings 6:12 NLT). God was revealing the plots, plans, and strategies of the enemy to a man of God for the people of God. This was not a good time to be a part of the kingdom of darkness. The kingdom of light (spiritual realm) always frustrates the kingdom of darkness (natural realm). The king demanded that his officers go and find where Elisha was living: "'Go and find out where he is,'" the king commanded, 'so I can send troops to seize him'" (2 Kings 6:13 NLT).

When they found out where Elisha was, they sent a report to the king; Elisha was in Dothan. "So one night the king of Syria *sent a great army* with *many chariots and horses* to surround the city" (2 Kings 6:14 NLT; emphasis added). Can you imagine what that must have looked like, a great army made up of many horses and chariots coming after one man?

The next morning Elisha's servant got up early and went outside. The first thing he saw was the massive army that had them surrounded. What he saw in the natural realm overpowered him. He panicked. He cried out, "Master, what in the world are we going to do now" (2 Kings 6:15 NKJV)? Elisha's response to his servant's cry doesn't make sense to the natural sense of hearing. "Don't be afraid!" Elisha told him. 'For there are more on our side than on theirs'" (2 Kings 6:16 NLT)! What? Was Elisha just using hyperbole in an attempt to calm the fear of his servant, or could it be that Elisha knew something that his servant didn't know? Maybe he saw something that his servant couldn't see.

Elisha prayed for his servant: "'O Lord, open his eyes and let him see!' The Lord opened the young man's eyes, and when he looked up, he saw that the hillside around Elisha was filled with horses and chariots of fire" (2 Kings 6:17 NLT). What made the difference between panic and peace? The servant panicked because his natural sense of sight was set on the natural realm. Elisha was at peace because he chose to set his spiritual sight on the spiritual realm. Elisha was able to see what his servant saw, but he was also able to see what God saw. Elisha was in this world, but he was not of this world. "What shall we say about such wonderful things as these. If God is for us, who can ever be against us" (Romans 8:31 NLT).

This is the spiritual maturity that most believers never reach—the unseen realm becomes more real than the seen realm. We're not talking about denying reality; we're talking about embracing the truth. Never forget that whatever God says is reality. Here's what God says, "By faith we understand that the entire universe was formed at God's command, that *what we now see did not come from anything that can be seen*" (Hebrews 11:3 NLT; emphasis added). Again we're left with only one conclusion. If what we can see was not made out of what we can see, then what we can see was made out of what we can't see. That's what God says, and whatever He says is reality.

Born from Above

Every person who has ever been born has a birth date. Most of us can tell you the day and year we were born. I say most, because the older you get, sometimes the memory gets a little foggy. We keep track of our age by how many celebrations we have of our days of birth. It was our physical birth that determined our identities as a human being. Growing up is simply maturing into that in which we were born. Maturity may help us in a lot of ways, but it doesn't make us more human. Our births determined that. Our physical identities come from being born from below.

We had a second birthday when we were born again. When Jesus told Nicodemus that he had to be born again in order to see the kingdom of God, He literally said unless you are born from above, you shall not see the kingdom of God (John 3:3 NKJV). Just like we get our natural identities from being born from below, we get our spiritual identities from being born from above. Our spiritual identities are determined by our births, our born-from-above experiences. This is so crucial to understanding our identities as children of God. Far too many believers are burning themselves out trying to become what they already are. We've been led to believe that the more we know and the more we do will make us more spiritual. Christian disciplines are wonderful, and they do have their places. But they can't make you more spiritual. What they are designed to do is mature us in what we already are, not to become what our spiritual birth has already determined.

We are spiritual beings living in this world in physical bodies. If we see ourselves as physical beings who have spirits, we will try to find our identities from the natural, seen, realm. That is a sure recipe for frustration and failure in living a victorious Christian life. We will never reign in this life if we don't know our new creation identities in Christ (Romans 5:17 NKJV). We are the recipients of a great exchange.

5

THE SOUL:
MIND, EMOTION, AND WILL

"Now may the God of peace Himself sanctify you completely; and may your whole *spirit, soul and body* be preserved blameless at the coming of our Lord Jesus Christ. He who calls you is faithful, who also will do it" (1 Thessalonians 5:23–24 NKJV; emphasis added). This verse describes a believer as being tripartite. A person has three parts, a spirit, a soul, and a body. We are spirit beings who have a soul, and we each live in a body. We are not physical beings having a temporary spiritual experience. We are spiritual beings having a temporary physical experience.

The Soul of Man
The Greek word for soul is *psuche*. The soul is made up of the mind, emotion, and will. The mind is the way we think. Emotion is how we feel, and the will is what we do. This is a very simplistic definition of the soul. Hebrews 4 says, "For the word of God is living and powerful, and sharper than any two-edged sword, piercing even to the division of *soul and spirit*" (Hebrews 4:12 NKJV; emphasis added). Sometimes

it's extremely difficult to distinguish between the soul and the spirit. In the Old Testament these two words are used interchangeably. Because of this interchange, many hold the dichotomous position that a person is a two-part being having a soul and a body. The soul and the spirit are similar in their natures and in their activities. Generally speaking, the spirit is the higher element that connects us to God. The soul is the lower element, the seat of our senses, desires, affections, and appetites. The spirit may be recognized as the life principle bestowed on a person by God, and the soul as the resulting life constituted in the individual. The body is much easier to define. It's the physical element of a person that is animated by the soul and the spirit. You remove the soul and the spirit from the body, and it returns to worm food. When God formed the body out of the dust from the ground, it did absolutely nothing (Genesis 2:7 NKJV). The body can't know God, love God, or serve God. The body became animated when God breathed His life into it. The body is the house that a person lives in that makes them legal to be here on the earth. When the spirit and soul leave the body at death, the person can't stay here. Without the body, they're no longer legal to be in the physical realm. *"Absent from the body* present with the Lord" (2 Corinthians 5:8 NKJV; emphasis added). The body is also the temple of the Holy Spirit (1Corinthians 6:19 NKJV).

Soul Exchange

The first Adam made an exchange that took place in a garden, the garden of Eden. Adam exchanged life for death. His disobedience gave way to sin, and sin gave life to death. The first Adam died spirit, soul, and body. That exchange moved him from being spirit-conscious to self-conscious. He could only then relate to the natural seen realm with his soul. Not only is Adam in the world, he's now of the world.

The last Adam, Jesus, made an exchange that took place in a garden, the garden of Gethsemane. He exchanged death for life. His obedience took the sting out of sin and life out of death. The last Adam died spirit, soul, and body. That exchange moves us from being self-conscious to being spirit-conscious. We can now relate to both the natural and the spiritual realms in our souls. We are in the world, but we are not of the world (John 17:15–16 NKJV).

The Way We Think: The Mind of the Soul

We should never underestimate the creative power of our thought lives. How we think will determine how we feel, our emotions. How we feel will influence what we do, our wills. Stinky thinking will ultimately lead to stinky living. If you are really serious about setting a new course for living your life, start with your thought life. Our lifestyles are determined by the way we think. Ralph Waldo Emerson's, "Plant a thought reap a word. Plant a word reap an action. Plant an action reap a habit. Plant a habit reap a character. Plant a character reap a destiny," may be one of the greatest quotes of all time. A person's destiny begins with a thought. Could this be why Paul says, "*Bring every thought captive* to the obedience of Christ" (2 Corinthians 10:5 NKJV; emphasis added).

I'm sure you've seen plaques and posts that say, "Our behavior determines who we are." That's a great saying, and I certainly understand what it implies. Actions can speak louder than words. Our behaviors do say a lot, but they don't determine who we are. Our behaviors reveal what we think and believe about ourselves. Our identities are determined by birth, not by our behaviors.

What we need is to bring our thinking in line with what the Word of God says, especially when it speaks to our identities as new creations: "And do not be conformed to this world but be transformed by *the renewing of your mind*, that you may prove what is that good and acceptable and perfect will of God" (Romans 12:2 NKJV; emphasis added). The renewing of your mind is to change the way you think. As a new creation in Christ, you now have that ability. It's possible to change the way we think, and once that happens, our behaviors will drastically be different. When we think about sin the way God thinks about sin, we will find ourselves taking fewer steps of stupid. We won't be sinless, but we will sin less. What makes the difference? The way we think about sin.

The moment we had our born-from-above experience with Christ we became new creations. There was an exchange of the soul. The soul is how we think, how we feel, and what we do. The way we think produces feelings, and our feelings are expressed through actions. So if we want to do better, we need to think better. We are capable of thinking differently than the way the world thinks. We have been given the ability to evaluate everything because we have the mind of Christ (1 Corinthians 2:10–16). We can take something in the natural realm and judge it in accordance with the truth of the spiritual realm. We do this by capturing our thoughts.

To live differently you must think differently, and that's been made possible through the exchanged life that Christ made for us. God gave His Son's life for our lives so we can have His life. We have the mind of Christ. So the ability to think differently is possible (1 Corinthians 2:16 NKJV). New creation thinking will begin to express itself through our characters (inside) and our conduct (outside).

A thought cannot live unless it's spoken. Once we speak a thought, we give life to it. *"Death and life are in the power of the tongue"* (Proverbs 18:21 NKJV; emphasis added). The enemy will lie and try to convince you that since you thought it, you might as well speak it. Don't fall for his lie.

How We Feel: The Emotions of the Soul

Feelings may be real, but that doesn't mean they're true. Feelings can be fickle. Therefore, they must be constantly monitored by the Word of God. I can feel that God doesn't love me, but that's certainly not the truth. As a matter of fact, God's not mad at you; He's madly in love with you. The enemy of your soul is very crafty at manipulating your feelings. If he can manipulate you in to thinking that no one likes you, it will affect the way you feel about people. The way you feel about a person will determine the way you treat that person. You may find it difficult to trust anyone. If a relationship is based on feelings, it's a ticking time bomb. It's not *if* it blows up, it's *when*. We are called to live by faith, not by our feelings (Hebrews 11:6 NKJV).

We should never deny our feelings. But at the same time, we should always examine them in the light of God's truth. His Word is truth (John 17:17 NKJV). It's very dangerous to make decisions, especially major decisions, based on feelings alone.

Feelings are not fundamental to faith. If you pray when you feel like praying, how often do you think you'll pray? If you share Christ with others based on how you feel, how often do you think you'll share Christ? If you read the Word of God when you feel like it, how much time do you think you'll spend in the Word? When you do the right thing, even when you don't feel like it, before long you may find yourself wanting to do the right thing. Feelings change. God gifted us with feelings as gauges to monitor what's going on in and around us, not as guides to order our steps. Emotions make a terrible boss.

"*Set you mind on things above*, not on things on the earth" (Colossians 3:2 NKJV; emphasis added). One translation says for us to think about the things of heaven, not the things on the earth. Set your thinking on things above, not on things below. We are spiritual beings living in a physical world. We're in the world, but not of the world. Our born-from-above experience with Christ allows us to access both the physical and the spiritual realms. As new creations, Christ has taken us from being self-conscious to being spirit-conscious. Thinking that's in line with your spiritual identity does not come easily or naturally. It must be intentional, done on purpose. Feelings are the fruit produced by our thinking. When we choose to set our thoughts on things above, our feelings will begin to line up with our thinking.

Over the years I've ministered to many Christians who struggle with low self-esteem. Even though it's not true, they feel they don't have much, if any, worth. Their feelings are real, but they're not true. What does a person do when they feel this way? They need to set their mind on the truth. What is truth? The Word of God is truth. "You made all the delicate, inner parts of my body and knit me together in my mother's womb. Thank you for making me so wonderfully complex! *Your workmanship is marvelous*—how well I know it" (Psalm 139:13–14 NLT; emphasis added). You may feel worthless, but the truth is, you are an incredible creation. You are His marvelous workmanship. God created you, and He doesn't waste His time on needless projects. Allow truth to define you, not your emotions and feelings.

> And now, dear brothers and sisters, one final thing. *Fix your thoughts on what is true,* and honorable, and right, and pure, and lovely, and admirable. *Think about things* that are excellent and worthy of praise. (Philippians 4:8 NKJV; emphasis added)

What We Do: The Will of the Soul

What you do does not determine who you are. What you do reveals what you believe about yourself. Our identities are determined by our births, not by our behaviors. It's time we come into agreement with the Word of God. I'm a Kniffen by birth. I can act in a way that's not congruent with the Kniffen name. When I do, I'm still a Kniffen because my behavior did not make me a Kniffen. My birth determined that. I didn't do anything to get myself into the Kniffen family, and there's nothing I can do to take myself out of the Kniffen family. I will always have the Kniffen DNA. If we start believing right, we just may start behaving right.

What you do reveals what you think about yourself. Remember, thoughts produce feelings, and feelings are expressed through actions.

If your understanding of the new creation is that you are only a sinner saved by grace, you will find it fairly easy to default to sinful behavior. A person usually lives up to their identity.

As a new creation in Christ, you are in the world. That's a fact. As a new creation in Christ, you are not of the world. That's the truth. You live in the natural realm, but your identity as a new creation is determined by the spiritual realm. You are a spirit being who has a soul, and you live in a body. Your body gives you access to this world, the natural, seen, realm. Your spirit gives you access to the spiritual, unseen, realm. Because you are a spiritual being, you can live in the world and not be of the world. How is this reality fleshed out? "I say then, *walk in the Spirit,* and you shall not fulfill the lust of the flesh" (Galatians 5:16 NKJV; emphasis added). Walking in the Spirit is not some mystical, abstract concept. It's allowing the Holy Spirit to be your guide for living life while you're in this world. If we allow the Spirit of God to guide us in our daily living, then we won't be giving in to fleshly cravings. What we do will be in character with who we are.

As God's children we have access to both the natural and the spiritual realms. We may be living in this world for the moment, but our citizenship is in heaven (Philippians 3:20 NKJV). The benefit of heavenly citizenship is a life of love, joy, peace, long-suffering, kindness, goodness, faithfulness, gentleness, and self-control (Galatians 5:22–23 NKJV). The way we enjoy the benefits that come with our heavenly citizenship is to live every day allowing the Holy Spirit to order our steps. It's fleshing out in our daily living our spiritual identities by the way we think, how we feel, and what we do. The fruit of the Spirit cannot be experienced by someone who does not have access to the spiritual realm. The things of the Spirit are kept and reserved for God's new creations. To be a new creation, you must have a born-from-above experience with Jesus Christ. The world is feverishly chasing after the quality of life that the King has already provided for His kids. Living out your identity as a new creation is the only way you can experience the fruit of the Spirit you have in the heavenly realm while you're living in the earthly realm.

We do what we do because we believe what we believe. When we start believing right, we'll start behaving right. When you made the exchange, you gave your life to Christ, and He gave His life to you. You became an entirely new creation, God's quid pro quo. You now have the ability to do what you could never do before you belonged to Christ. You can reign in this life. It's time to start living up to your new identity in Christ.

6

THE IDENTITY OF A TRUE BELIEVER

People who attend church for any length of time will become bilingual. They will talk normally during the week, but once they walk through the doors of the church building on Sunday, they start speaking a whole new language. It's called Christianese. Christianese is the insider language that church people speak, and it may sound confusing to the uninitiated non-Christian. I call it pious pontification.

Talking the talk has become more important for many people than walking the walk. If it sounds like a Christian, smells like a Christian, and looks like a Christian, it must be a Christian. Is the true identity of a believer determined by appearance, or is it much deeper than that? A person may say they have faith, so that proves they are true believers. Maybe, maybe not. It depends on what kind of faith a person is operating in. There are three kinds of faith: There is historical faith, crisis faith, and saving faith. It's crucial that we understand the differences. Where we spend eternity is at stake.

Historical Faith

Let's take George Washington as an example. I think most sane people believe that George Washington really existed. Even though we've never met George Washington, we're convinced he was a real person. History books record the fact that George Washington was one of the Founding Fathers of the United States and served as the first president from 1789 to 1797. Even though we've never received a telephone call or a text message from George Washington, we believe in him. That's historical faith. Many believe in Jesus the same way. They have faith in Jesus, but it's historical faith. Even demons believe Jesus is real (James 2:19 NKJV).

Crisis Faith

Crisis faith is when we get serious with God. Our faith moves from our heads to our hearts, from historical faith to crisis faith. Our emotions are in the mix now. Sometimes during these times of crisis we make deals with God that we don't follow through on. "Lord, you get me out of this and I will _____." You fill in the blank. During times of crisis, it's easy to write checks with our mouths that we never intend to cash. When the crisis passes, so does our faith. Like historical faith, crisis faith won't cut the mustard.

Saving Faith

Saving faith is when we place our hope, confidence, and lives in God's hands. We believe *into* Jesus. It's all Jesus, or we're sunk. The values of our faith is determined by the objects of our faith. Saving faith is trusting God with our lives. It's a matter of life and death. The following story may help you understand what trusting in Jesus with your life looks like.

The Wheelbarrow

You are visiting Niagara Falls. You notice that a wire has been strung over the Falls connecting one side of the Falls to the opposite side. A man is standing there with a wheelbarrow, talking to a small crowd of people who have gathered. He asks the group if they believe he can push the wheelbarrow on the wire to the other side and back. No one answers. How's it possible to know if he can do what he says he can do?

The man gets on the wire with his wheelbarrow and pushes it to the other side and back. Then he says to the crowd, "How many of you think I can push this wheelbarrow to the other side and back?" What do you think their answer would be? They know he can pull it off because they saw him do it. Then he asks another question: "How many of you believe that I can push you in this wheelbarrow to the other side and back?" How will you ever know? You'll have to get *into* the wheelbarrow and trust his ability to do what he says he can do. Your life is totally in his hands. That's what it means to trust *in* Jesus as your Lord and Savior.

Christ in Us—Us in Christ

I'm told by sources I trust that for every time you see the words, "Christ is in us," there are ten verses that say, "We are in Christ." That's a ten-to-one ratio. Our identities as believers come from who we are *in Christ*. Jesus said, "At that day you will know that *I am in My Father, and you in Me, and I in you*" (John 14:20 NKJV; emphasis added). Since Jesus is in the Father, we're in Jesus, and Jesus is in us; then we're in both Jesus and the Father. Philip asked Jesus to show them the Father. The answer Jesus gives Philip is key to understanding our identities as children of God: "Have I been with you so long, and yet you have not known Me, Phillip? He who has seen Me has seen the Father; so how can you say, 'Show us the Father'? Do you not believe that *I am in the Father*, and *the Father in Me*? The words that I speak to you I do not speak on My own authority; but the Father who dwells in Me does the works. Believe Me, that *I am in the Father* and *the Father in Me,* or else believe Me for the sake of the works themselves" (John 14:9–11 NKJV; emphasis added). God the Father was living His life through Jesus, as Jesus. That's how we walk out our faith as true believers. We allow Jesus to live His life through us, as us.

When people tell me that living the Christian life is hard, I tell them that it's not only hard, it's impossible. It's impossible to live life under the law, and it's impossible to live life under grace. If you could live out the requirements of the law—which are personal, perpetual, perfection—you would have to be God. If you could live a life of grace, you wouldn't need God. How in the world, then, do we live out our new creation identities? We let Jesus live His life through us, as us, just like the Father lived His life through Jesus, as Jesus.

We Will Get Our Identities from the World or from the Word

Why is it so difficult for a child of God to say and believe, "I am who I Am says I am? If we don't allow the Word of God to tell us who we are as believers, I assure you the world will have no problem telling us. We'll get our identities from the world or from the Word.

After Jesus spent forty days being tempted by the devil, He returned to Nazareth, the town where He grew up. Since it was the Sabbath, He went to the synagogue. For the Sabbath reading, Jesus was asked to read from the book of Isaiah. He opened the book to where the last reader had ended. He began, "The Spirit of the Lord is upon *Me,* because He has anointed *Me* to preach the gospel to the poor; He has sent *Me* to heal the brokenhearted, to proclaim liberty to the captives and recovery of sight to the blind, to set at liberty those who are oppressed; to proclaim the acceptable year of the Lord" (Isaiah 62:1–2 NKJV; emphasis added). I find it interesting that He didn't read the last part of verse 2: "And the day of the vengeance of our God." The day of God's vengeance had not come yet. It was a day of God's grace.

Jesus closed the book, handed it back to the synagogue attendant, and sat down. Jesus said to those in attendance, *"Today this Scripture is fulfilled in your hearing"* (Luke 4:21 NKJV; emphasis added). Jesus told the synagogue crowd that the prophet Isaiah was talking about Him. Pay close attention to what Jesus did. He found Himself in the scriptures. The living Word found Himself in the written Word. In the very next verse, the people asked, "Is this not Joseph's son?" (Luke 4:22 NKJV). They identified Him as the son of Joseph. If we don't allow the written Word to tell us who we are in Christ, the world will be more than happy to do it for us.

Life Below the Line Is Real: Life Above the Line Is True

To get a better understanding of my identity in Christ, I've found it very helpful to make a little chart. You can do this in your head, but I highly recommend you put it on paper so you can continually add to it as the Holy Spirit leads you. Draw a horizontal line. Above the line write the words, "spiritual unseen realm." Below the line write, "natural seen realm." The line is the demarcation between the two. Actually, there is no line separating the two realms, but for the sake of learning, the line helps immensely.

Everything below the line is real; everything above the line is true. Just because something is real doesn't necessarily make it true. Feelings are certainly real, but feelings may not be true. Above the line it's *us in Christ.* Below the line it's *Christ in us.* Above the line we are "complete in Christ" (Colossians 2:10 NKJV). Below the line we are being made complete: "Being confident of this very thing, that He who *has begun a good* work in you *will complete it* until the day of Jesus Christ" (Philippians 1:6 NKJV; emphasis added). Looks like we have a contradiction here. Are we complete, or are we being completed? When there appears to be a contradiction in Scripture, that's exactly what you have—an appearance.

This is the purpose for drawing the horizontal line separating the two realms. Above the line, spiritual realm, we are complete in Christ (Colossians 2:10 NKJV). Below the line, natural realm, we are becoming what we already are above the line (Philippians 1:6 NKJV). In the natural realm, we are becoming a mature example of what we already are in the spiritual realm. We are in Christ above the line, complete. Christ is in us below the line, and we're becoming complete. This is why Jesus said we're *in* the world, but we're not *of* the world. While we're in the world, our purpose is to flesh out who we are in the unseen, spiritual, realm. How do we do that? By allowing Christ to live His through us, as us, just like the Father lived His life through Jesus, as Jesus. "Love has been perfected among us in this: that we may have boldness in the day of judgment; because *as He is so are we* in this world" (I John 4:17 NKJV; emphasis added). We are in the natural realm what Jesus is in the spiritual realm.

This is your identity as a child of God, the *new you* in Christ. Jesus was in the Father above the line. The Father was in Jesus below the line (John 14:9–11, 20 NKJV). You are in Christ above the line; Christ is in you below the line.

The Divine Exchange: God's Quid Pro Quo

"For He (God) *made Him* (Jesus) *who knew no sin to be sin for us, that we might become the righteousness of God in Him"* (2 Corinthians 5:21 NKJV; emphasis added). How many sins did Jesus commit before He was made sin for us? Not one. How many righteous deeds did we do before we were made righteous? Not one (Ephesians 2:8–9 NKJV). This is the exchange that God made for us in Christ. Jesus was made what I was so that I could become what He is. My sinful disobedience was overpowered and negated by His sinless obedience. What I was, He was made so that what He is I became. That's the identity of a true believer.

7

THE MIRACLE OF BEING BORN, FROM ABOVE

How do you explain a miracle? If it were possible to explain, it wouldn't be a miracle. Can you imagine how difficult and awkward it must have been for Mary when she tried to explain to Joseph that the child she was carrying was from God? How do you explain a miracle so someone can understand it? Trying to explain a miracle is like trying to explain the inexplicable or unscrutinizing the inscrutable. It just ain't going to happen.

How do you understand a miracle? If it were possible to understand, it wouldn't be a miracle. Put yourself in Joseph's sandals. He's trying to understand what Mary said about how she got pregnant, but it's beyond human comprehension. Since a miracle can't be explained or understood, how is Joseph going to know the truth. An angel of the Lord appeared to Joseph in a dream and confirmed the validity of Mary's testimony: "But while he (Joseph) thought about these things, behold, an *angel of the Lord appeared to him in a dream*, saying, 'Joseph, son of David, do not be afraid to take to you Mary your wife, for *that which is conceived in her is of the Holy Spirit'"* (Matthew 1:20 NKJV; emphasis added).

Spiritually Wired

How do you explain to someone what it means to be born from above so they can understand it? The new life we have in Christ is a miracle, so it's impossible to explain. It takes a revelation. A revelation is a divine or supernatural disclosure. As a new creation in Christ, we are spiritually wired to receive information from the Spirit of God, who abides within us. The Holy Spirit communicates with our spirits. He's called the Spirit of truth (John 16:13 NKJV). He knows everything about everything and has promised to teach us all things. The Holy Spirit is the only One who can give us a *reveal*-ation.

Have you ever shared your salvation experience with someone who doesn't know Christ and have them look at you with that "vacancy sign" stare? The person may even be smiling, but you know in your knower the person is not home. Most of us probably have. The next time this happens, picture Joseph in your mind, listening to Mary telling him about her pregnancy. A person listening to your testimony may actually have a desire to understand what you're saying but is not spiritually wired for it.

Then there are those who respond with sarcasm and mockery when they hear you share your born-from-above experience. What you're saying doesn't appear foolish to them, it *is* foolish. "But the *natural man* (unsaved) *does not receive the things of the Spirit of God,* for *they are foolishness to him; nor can he know the,* because *they are spiritually discerned*" (1 Corinthians 2:14 NKJV; added). A person without Christ is not spiritually wired to receive or discern the things of God.

Reveal-ation of Being Born from Above

As a child of God, we do not have the ability—nor have we been given the responsibility—to give anyone a revelation, no matter how badly we may want to. That's the work and ministry of the Holy Spirit. When we tell others what Christ has done for us, we are sharing information. That's our responsibility, and it's something we have the ability to do. The Holy Spirit can then take that information and bring about a supernatural disclosure, a divine unveiling to someone. A revelation is not given just so we will have a revelation. Only the Lord knows how many revelations He's given us that we've done absolutely nothing with. God has a purpose behind every revelation that He gives.

Transformation of Being Born from Above

The purpose behind a revelation is transformation. Transformation is something that takes place on the *inside,* and then it manifests itself on the *outside.* The Greek word for transformation means to "change forms." It literally means to go through a process that produces a new form. An illustration of transformation would be a caterpillar becoming a butterfly. A caterpillar weaves and enters a cocoon and then comes out a butterfly. What was a caterpillar is now a totally new creation; what is now seen on the outside is a manifestation of the transformation that took place on the inside. There has been an exchange. A caterpillar has been exchanged for a butterfly.

Manifestation of Being Born from Above

Manifestation is walking the exchanged life, the life that has been transformed by the power of God. Until there is a walking out of what's been worked in, then all we have is information. As long as information stays in our heads, we are in possession of it. When it makes the shift from our heads to our hearts, it now has us. A revelation comes into our spirits and is intended to pass through our feet. When we start walking what we've been given, the information has us. This new transformed life will manifest through our characters and our conduct.

Confrontation of Being Born from Above

From information to revelation there will always be confrontation. This clash is an attempt by the enemy of our souls to keep revelation from ever manifesting in our lives. This battle will come from without or from within, but it will come. The enemy doesn't care how much spiritual revelation we possess as long as it doesn't possess us. He doesn't care how full our heads are with Bible knowledge as long as we do nothing with it.

Exchanged Life: Information

The Word of God divides humankind into two categories: the natural person and the spiritual person (1 Corinthians 2:14–16 NKJV). The natural person is the individual who's never had a second birthday. They haven't been born again. They may know about God, even acknowledge God, but don't know Him. The natural individual can be a good person with high morals or a bad person with low morals. What makes a person natural is their spiritual condition; they have not been born from above. The only birth they've had is from below, in the natural realm. Birth determined their identity.

The spiritual person, on the other hand, has said yes to Jesus. They have accepted and received His invitation to life. The spiritual person has had a second birthday. They are now spiritually wired to receive from God. They know about God, but more important, they know God. A spiritual person is still in the world, but they're not of the world. Birth determined their identity.

Being a Christian is not about *getting religion*. This new life we have as children of God is much more than a life that's been changed. It's a life that's been exchanged (2 Corinthians 5:17–21 NKJV). We surrendered our lives to the Lord, and in exchange, He gave us His life. Using our earlier illustration, we could say it this way: We were caterpillars, but now we're butterflies.

Exchanged Life: Revelation

"Therefore, if anyone is *in Christ, he is a new creation; old things have passed away*; behold, *all things have become new*" (2 Corinthians 5:17 NKJV; emphasis added). As children of God, we are brand-new creations. We bear our heavenly Father's DNA. Birth determined our identities. Our first birth determines our natural identities; our second birth determines our spiritual identities. Behavior had nothing to do with establishing our identities.

Our new life came from an exchange: *"God was in Christ reconciling* (exchanging) *the world to Himself"* (2 Corinthians 5:19 NKJV; emphasis added). Because your old nature was exchanged for a new nature, you have an entirely new identity. The exchange took you from being a sinner to being a saint, from being unholy to holy, from being unrighteous to being righteous. Jesus was made what we were so we could be what He is (2 Corinthians 5:21 NKJV). The exchange not only took care of who we were (sinful nature), it took care of what we did (sinful behavior).

Our new life is in God's Son. Jesus said that those who believe in Him will be given everlasting life, a life that has no end (John 6:47 NKJV). He also said that those who trust in Him will have eternal life, a life that has no beginning (John 6:54 NKJV). A life that has no beginning has no past. The new you has no past. That in no way does it imply we won't have to deal with the consequences from the choices we made before we were new creations or have to deal with the fallout from fleshly choices we make as believers. I'm convinced that the more we know about our identities in Christ, the less steps of stupid we'll take.

> Love has been perfected among us in this: that we may have boldness in the day of judgment, *because as He is, so are we in this world.* (1 John 4:17 JKJ; emphasis added)

> And because of His glory and excellence, He has given us great and precious promises. These are the promises that enable *you to share His divine nature* and escape the world's corruption caused by human desires. (2 Peter 1:4 NLT; emphasis added)

Exchanged Life: Transformation

The new birth experience is an inside-out work of the Holy Spirit. This transformation, which takes place on the inside of a person, is an exchange of natures. The old you has been exchanged for a new you. This makes it possible for you to think differently, feel differently, and act differently. Whatever is on the inside will eventually make its way to the outside.

Your salvation experience is supernatural. I use this term to draw a distinction between the natural and the spiritual. Since your new life is supernatural, it can't be supported by natural means. This is why so many believers become disgruntled, disappointed, and discouraged. They've been convinced this new life can and must be sustained by works; that is, getting and keeping God's approval depends on all the good things we do. How many good deeds did you do to be accepted by God? If you're still thinking about it, I'll give you the answer—none! You didn't do anything to get your new identity, and you can't do anything to lose your new identity. We were created human beings, not human doings. Yes, we do good deeds, but the good deeds we do, come out of our beings, our new natures. We don't *do good* in order to *be good.*

A group of folks came to Jesus one day with a question about doing the works of God. His response is insightful: "Then they said to Him, 'What shall we do that we may work the works of God?' Jesus answered and said to them, 'This is *the work of God,* that *you believe* in Him whom He sent'" (John 6:28–29 NKJV; emphasis added). The work that God requires from us is to *believe* Him.

We are not new creations because of our good works, but we were created for good works. "For *by grace you have been saved* through faith and that not of yourselves, *it is the gift of God, not of works,* lest anyone should boast. For we are His workmanship, *created in Christ Jesus for good works,* which *God prepared beforehand* that *we should walk in them*" (Ephesians 2:8–10 NKJV; emphasis added). Pay close attention to what Paul says in this verse. We were saved because of God's grace, not because of our good works. Salvation is not a reward for all the good things we have done, so we have nothing to boast about. As we live out our new creation identities on a daily basis, we'll find ourselves doing right because we're believing right.

Exchanged Life: Manifestation

If a legitimate transformation has taken place in a person's life, there will be an outward manifestation of it. That's the purpose for receiving a revelation. We can't see the miracle that took place on the inside of an individual, but we can see the fruit of it on the outside. The manifestation proves the transformation was real. Manifestation is bringing into the seen realm what took place in the unseen realm. Transformation without manifestation remains only information. The new creation life will express itself through our attitudes and our actions.

Since the transformation—exchange—of a soul is a miracle, it can neither be seen with the physical eye nor understood by the natural mind. That's why it's called a miracle. It's not explicable by natural or scientific laws. The results of a miracle can be observed. What happened to an individual when they accepted Christ as their

Lord and Savior will manifest through their lifestyle. Even though it took place in the invisible realm, it will manifest in the visible realm. This is the purpose of receiving a revelation. It was given to bring about a transformation that leads ultimately to a manifestation, a walking out of what's been worked in.

Jesus had the ability to take the simply profound and make it profoundly simple. In one of His teaching moments He said, "For *all that is secret* will eventually be *brought into the open,* and *everything that is concealed* will be *brought to light and made known to all*" (Luke 8:17 NLT; emphasis added). Secret sin on earth is an open scandal in heaven. Jesus is giving us the principle of exposure: Everything that's been done in secret, will have its day in the light. It's just a matter of time.

Let's take this principle of exposure and apply it to the miracle of being born from above. In the secret place, inaccessible to the natural eye, a transformation took place. The old soul was exchanged for a new soul. The old you became a new you. There will be a manifestation of that transformation. What was done in secret will be made known.

Exchanged Life: Confrontation

As noted previously, between the information given and the revelation received there will be confrontation. Truth will always be challenged by a lie. This confrontation will come from within or from without, but it will come. The challenge from within will be our thinking, our presuppositions. The challenge that comes from without will come from those around us who have their own presuppositions. It's rare to find someone who believes what they believe because it was hammered out on the anvil of diligent personal Bible study.

There are incredible benefits that come from sitting at the feet of a person who can help us grow and mature as a child of God. We'll never get to the place where we'll not need instruction in righteousness. Discovering our identities as new creations in Christ will be a lifetime pursuit. In the chase for understanding, we must never forget that we have the best teacher we will ever have residing within us, the Holy Spirit.

All of us have a penchant to embrace whatever matches our experiences, even to the exclusion of what the scriptures may say about it. Just take a glance at the verses you have underlined or highlighted in your Bible. I would wager the largest percentage of them are those that support what you believe. By no means am I suggesting you've violated any principles of hermeneutics by doing so. Here's the point I'm making. Unknowingly, the motivation behind our Bible reading is to find passages that will support what we believe. Our incentives should be to find out what the Word of God says and then demand that our experiences rise to that level.

The enemy of our soul is called a thief by Jesus. He's faithful to his job description given in John 10: "The purpose of the thief is to *steal* and to *kill* and to *destroy*" (John 10:10 NKJV; emphasis added). Satan is a thief, and what do thieves do? They steal. What's he out to steal? Your identity. If he's successful in stealing your identity, then he can kill your confidence and destroy your hope. He's very skilled in using feelings and facts to support his lies. The thief will try and convince you that since your feelings are real, they must be true. Facts are facts, so they can't be denied. What he doesn't want us to know is that truth trumps feelings and facts every time. When feelings and facts come into competition with God's truth, truth always wins.

We find another job description given in John 10: "I (Jesus) *have come that they may have life, and that they may have it* (life) *more abundantly*" (John 10:10 NKJV; emphasis added). Jesus is always faithful to His job description.

8

FREEDOM OF THE EXCHANGED LIFE

A life that's been exchanged is free to enjoy the birthright benefits that come with being a child of God. This is the abundant life that Jesus offers to anyone who will receive His invitation to life (John 10:10 NKJV). To be in the family of God has incredible benefits. These benefits cannot be enjoyed if we don't know who we are as new creations. Ignorance may not be bliss after all. It can be very costly.

Freedom from Sin, not Free to Sin

Sometimes people confuse freedom from sin as a license to sin. It's actually the opposite. When you know you're really free, you lose your taste for sin. Your *want to* no longer wants to sin. Anyone who thinks that once the exchange has been made they are free to live anyway they choose has not experienced the exchange. If there's been a legitimate transformation, there will be a manifestation. When you give your life to Christ, and in return He gives you His life, your want tos are no longer the same.

I'm deeply in love with my wife. Apart from my salvation experience, she's the best thing that's ever happened to me. I'm not faithful to her because she would take a contract out on me if I wasn't. I'm faithful to her because I know how much she loves me. Her commitment to me and love for me over the years we've been married are unquestioned. I'm faithful to her because I know how much she loves me. I wouldn't want to abuse or violate her trust in any form or fashion. I wouldn't want to do anything purposely to bring pain to her heart.

The same is true with being a child of God. When you know how madly in love with you the Lord is, you'll have no desire to use the benefits of your birthright as an excuse to sin. The enemy has convinced many to believe that if they embrace and receive God's amazing grace, it will give them a permit to sin. That's a lie from the thief. People sin all the time without a permit. The only way to lose one's appetite for sin is God's grace. The freedom of the exchanged life is to be free from sin, not free to sin.

Freedom from the Pressure of Performance

The thief is after our identities. He's had measured success in convincing us that in order to be accepted by God and to stay in His favor we have to perform. The more we do and the better we do it, the more God will love us. We're OK with that as long as we have our A game, but on the days, weeks, and months when we can't find our games, it's a different story. Our acceptance is not based on what we can do for Him but on what He's done for us. The exchanged life is all about Him. If the enemy can get us to shift our focuses away from Jesus Christ, we're no longer talking about the exchanged life.

If we choose to live our lives based on performance, then God will require personal, perpetual perfection. No pressure! If we choose to live our lives under grace, then Christ will provide for us. He fulfilled the performance requirement of the law: "For what the law could not do in that it was weak through the flesh, God did by sending His own Son in the likeness of sinful flesh, on account of sin He condemned sin in the flesh, that *the righteous requirement of the law* might be fulfilled *in us* who do not walk according to the flesh but according to the Spirit" (Romans 8:3–4 NKJV; emphasis added). The righteous requirement of the law was not fulfilled by us. It was fulfilled by Jesus who lives His life in us. He did what we couldn't do, so we could be what we couldn't be, so we could have what we didn't have.

Freedom Comes from Intimacy with the Truth

I'm sure most of us have said or have heard it said that the truth shall set you free. That's usually said in an attempt to get someone to fess up to something. To give it more punch we may say, "The Bible says the truth shall set you free." Yes and no. The Word of God is true whether we're free or not. Actually, the Bible says it's the *truth you know* that sets you free. To *know,* means more than just having a head full of information. It's not giving mental assent to something. It's a word for intimacy. "Adam *knew* Eve his wife, and *she conceived* and bore Cain" (Genesis 4:1 NKJV; emphasis added). Being intimate with the Word of God is what gives birth to freedom.

"Then Jesus said to those Jews who believed Him 'If you *abide in My word*, you are My disciples indeed. And you shall *know the truth*, and *the truth shall make you free*" (John 8:31-32 NKJV; emphasis added). To abide means to settle down and make yourself at home. The more intimate we become with the written Word (Bible), the more we'll know the living Word (Jesus). The more intimate we are with the living Word, the more freedom we'll enjoy. The better we know Him, the better we'll understand the liberty we've been given in the exchanged life.

Knowing truth is knowing God because God is truth (Deuteronomy 32:4; Psalm 31:5; Isaiah 65:16 NKJV). Truth is God expressing Himself. Whatever God is, He is completely. Since He's truth, He's the complete truth. When Jesus said, "I am the way, the truth, and the life. No one comes to the Father except through Me"

(John 14:6 NKJV; emphasis added), He was revealing His identity. Jesus was God in the flesh.

Wherever the Spirit of the Lord Is, There's Freedom

"For the Lord is the Spirit, and *wherever the Spirit of the Lord is, there is freedom*" (2 Corinthians 3:17 NKJV; emphasis added). As a new creation, the Spirit of the Lord dwells in you. You are God's home, His permanent residence. You're not His vacation home, where He comes and stays for a few days during the year, when He takes time off from His busy schedule. "Do you not know that you are the temple of God and that *the Spirit of God dwells in you?*" (1 Corinthians 3:16 NKJV; emphasis added). When you made the exchange, you surrendered your old life to Him, and in the exchange, He gave you a totally new life. God moved into the new you as His permanent residence.

Wherever the Spirit of the Lord is, there's liberty (2 Corinthians 3:17 NKJV). Since the Spirit of the Lord lives within us, why aren't more Christians enjoying the freedom that comes with the exchanged life? I think the reasons are limited. It could be we just don't believe it. Our experiences don't match up with the Word (truth), so we go with our experiences. Maybe we don't know the freedom we have in Christ because we've never been taught. This is why it's so important for us to spend time in the written Word; it will bring us face-to-face with the living Word. "*Therefore, if the Son makes you free you shall be free indeed*" (John 8:36 NKJV; emphasis added).

The longing of every soul is to be free. Freedom can't be found in anything or in anyone other than Christ. When the Spirit of the Lord moved into your life, He brought freedom with Him. The exchanged life is His life in you. The way we live out this freedom is to allow Jesus to live His life through us the way the Father lived His life through Jesus. Jesus said, "Do you not believe that *I am in the Father*, and *the Father in Me?* The words that I speak to you I do not speak on My own authority; but *the Father who dwells in Me does the works.* Believe Me that I am in the Father and the Father in Me, or else believe Me for the sake of the works themselves" (John 14:10–11 NKJV; emphasis added).

Freedom Is not Based on Our Physical Circumstances

There are many incarcerated believers all around the world who are freer than many who are not locked up. Why is that? Freedom is not about physical circumstances; it's a spiritual condition. The freedom we have in Christ is not about what's happening on the outside. True freedom is about what's happened on the inside. This is why faith is lived from the inside out, not the outside in. The new creation life in Christ is not a style of living that's forever changing. It's a lifestyle that remains constant. It's walking out what's been worked in. It's an outward manifestation of an inward transformation.

There are millions of believers who suffer persecution for confessing Jesus as their Lord and Savior, yet they're free. Many have forfeited their physical freedom for openly expressing their faith in Christ. The body can be locked up, but you can't lock up the spirit. A believer who does not enjoy the freedom they have in Christ is like a person living in a cell with the door wide open.

"Therefore if the Son *makes* you free, you shall be *free indeed*" (John 8:36 NKJV; emphasis added). Not only has Jesus made us free, He has made us *really* free. Most believers embrace the theology of being free in Christ, but they're not experiencing the reality of that freedom. As a child of God, you have been freed from all the judgment and condemnation that the old you were under.

I read a short story about a man who was browsing through a farmers' market. He came upon a booth where a man had several quails tied together by a string. The birds were walking around a stake that had been driven into the ground. He asked if the birds were for sale. After negotiating a price, the man bought the birds and immediately began to cut the string that had them bound. The man who had sold the birds asked him why he was cutting the string. "To set the birds free," was the answer he got. Once the strings had been cut from the legs of the birds, they kept walking around the stake. He began to wave his hat at the birds, causing them to fly in all directions. They were free the moment the string was cut. When they flew away is when they were *really free*. Jesus not only cut the string and freed us, He allowed us to fly and experience what it's like to *really be free*.

The Contents of the Gift

Living as a captive when you've been set free is like accepting a gift but never opening it. You have the container, but you are not enjoying its contents. The gift was given so you could enjoy what's in it. Jesus is God's gift to us. When we accepted Jesus, we not only have the gift, we have the contents of the gift. Everything that God has to offer us is in His Son. Far too many have never opened the gift to see inside. We don't know what we've been given. Salvation is a gift from God that's full of incredible benefits. These benefits are wrapped up in Jesus Christ. Way too many believers never enjoy these benefits because they've never opened the gift.

In John 4, we have the story of Jesus and the Samaritan woman. Jesus is sitting on the well, talking with this woman who had come to draw water. When He asked her for a drink, she was stunned. She reminded him that Jews didn't have anything to do with Samaritans, especially Samaritan women. What Jesus said to her is worth paying attention to: "Jesus replied, '*If you only knew the gift God* has for you and Who you are speaking to, you would ask Me, and *I would give you living water*" (John 4:10 NLT; emphasis added). I love the words, "if you only knew." Jesus was telling this woman that God's gift to her was sitting right in front of her. He was the gift. What was inside the gift? What was inside the container? The very thing her thirsty soul was crying out for, living water.

Jesus is God's gift to us. A gift can't be earned, and a gift can't be sold. A gift is something that's given willingly to someone without payment. That's why it's called a gift. If we only knew what we have inside the gift. This is why Jesus said that if we would abide in His Word, if we remain faithful to His teachings, we will know truth, and the truth we come to know will result in freedom.

The Exchange of Natures

The exchanged life frees us from sin; it does not free us to sin. Because there's been an exchange of natures, the proclivity now is to live our lives in a way that brings honor and glory to our heavenly Father. We will stumble from time to time. Even though we're not of this world, we're still in this world, with all its diversions and distractions. We'll never be comfortable with sin anymore because it goes against our new natures.

Paul writes these words to the church in Rome: "But *you are not in the flesh* but *in the Spirit,* if indeed *the Spirit* of God *dwells in you.* Now if anyone does not have the Spirit of Christ, he is not one of His" (Romans 8:9 NKJV; emphasis added). If you are a child of God, you are in the Spirit, and the Spirit lives in you. If not, then you do not belong to Him. It's that simple. Before you accepted Christ as your Lord and Savior, you were in the flesh. Now that you've been born from above, you're in the Spirit.

When we take steps of stupid and do things that are not in sync with our new natures, we usually describe that misstep this way. "I got in the flesh." I think most of us understand what that means. We did or said something we're not proud of, something that's not becoming of a Christian. The truth is, once we're saved, we can never *get in* the flesh again. Being "in the flesh," and, "living by the flesh," are not synonymous terms. Before we had our born-from-above experience with Christ, we were in the flesh. We didn't move in and out of the Spirit because that was impossible. As new creations, we are in the Spirit, so we don't move in and out of the flesh. What we can do is set our minds on the flesh, and when we do, we may find ourselves living by the flesh, which is contrary to our new natures (Romans 8:5 NKJV). This is why we are to set our minds and affections on things above (Colossians 3:2 NKJV).

The exchanged life is the greatest quid pro quo that's ever been pulled off. Something for something, our old lives for new lives. This for that. You were given a new nature for your old nature. Christ exchanged His life for ours. "For He (God) made Him (Jesus) who knew no sin to be sin for us, that we might become the righteousness of God in Him" (2 Corinthians 5:21 NKJV). He was made what I was, so I can be what he is.

9

LIVING LIFE BY ANOTHER

The Christian language is filled with platitudes and proverbs that may have a biblical ring to them but can't be backed up by scripture. To give a platitude even more credence, it may be prefaced with, "The Bible says." Not many people want to challenge a statement that begins with, "The Bible says." After all, who wants to question or challenge God? There's a name for someone who wants to go toe-to-toe with Him—victim.

Does the Bible Say ...

"Cleanliness is next to godliness." I would say the odds are pretty good you've heard that said. If you had been raised by my mother, you certainly would have heard it, especially at bath time in the evening. "Son, go run your bathwater. Bathe good; use plenty of soap." Of course I would moan and complain; that's what young boys do. Country boys are allergic to water and soap. In response to my resistance, my mother would say in a soft, loving tone, "The Bible says, 'Cleanliness is next to godliness.'" My mother was unknowingly pitting me against God. I'm all in when it comes to good hygiene, but that adage is not in the Bible.

"The Lord will not put more on you than you can bear." Ever heard that one? Don't try and sell that to the apostle Paul. "We think you ought to know, dear brothers and sisters, about the trouble we went through in the province of Asia. We were crushed and overwhelmed beyond our ability to endure, and we thought we would never live through it" (2 Corinthians 1:8 NLT). It sounds to me like Paul knows something about hopeless situations. Here's a news flash. Sometimes God may allow situations to become more than we can bear. Somewhere along the road in life it's possible to find yourself in a situation that you can't handle. When this happens, it's not because God is mean or that He doesn't love you. The heavy burden that threatens to crush you just may be what the Lord uses to cause you to trust Him more. Life-threatening seasons may be our opportunities to find out how good God is and just how much He loves us. God may use the circumstance we thought we wouldn't live through to teach us how to live.

"God helps those who help themselves." If there's anything that gets my goat, it's laziness. That's one of my pet peeves. The Bible does say, "Even while we were with you, we gave you this command: *Those unwilling to work will not get to eat*" (2 Thessalonians 3:10 NLT; emphasis added). Paul is talking about those who are physically able to work but because of laziness, refuse to do so. This statement about God helping those who help themselves is usually said in an attempt to convince someone that for God to help you, you must make sure you've done all you possibly can. If you haven't done all you can do, don't expect God to step in and help. Don't even ask for His help; you're on your own.

Sometimes the best position we can find ourselves in is when we realize we can't do this. If we could do it, we wouldn't need God. Just because someone prefaces what they say with, "The Bible says," doesn't mean the Bible says, even if it has a familiar King James sound.

Christ Is Our Lives

What do you have that wasn't given to you by God? If we're honest, we can't name one thing that wasn't given to us by our Creator. That includes the breath in our lungs. Think about that the next time you inhale a breath of fresh air. Our existence is totally dependent on Him. This was God's design from the very beginning of time. He's the environment for our survival. There will always be people who'll never acknowledge this truth, but their denials don't change the truth.

Jesus underscores the truth of not being able to exist without Him in His teaching on the vine and the branches: "Remain in me, and I will remain in you. For a branch cannot produce fruit if it is severed from the vine, and you cannot be fruitful unless you remain in me. Yes, I am the vine, you are the branches. Those who remain in me, and I in them, will produce much fruit. *For apart from me you can do nothing*" (John 15:4–5 NLT; emphasis added). Jesus didn't say, "Apart from me there's not much you can do." He said, "You can't do anything apart from me. Anything!" There's no hope of doing anything without Christ.

Life with Christ is another story. "I can do all things through Christ who strengthens me" (Philippians 4:13 NKJV). The strength we have to do anything and everything comes from Christ. Without Him, we're sunk. This message is confirmed in Acts 17: "For in Him (Christ) we *live* and *move* and *have our being*" (Acts 17:28 NKJV; emphasis added). Without Christ it's impossible for us to exist. This begs the question again. What do we have that wasn't given to us by God? I think this passage we just quoted from the book of Acts answers that question for us—not one thing.

When you accepted Christ's invitation to life and received Jesus as your Lord and Savior, He gave you a completely new life. Your old life was exchanged for a new one. There's not a smidgen of your old life left that needs to be renovated, rededicated, or updated. Since Christ gave this new life to you, you can't live it without Him. God will never give you anything that you can do without Him. When we attempt to do something that's impossible for us to do, a disastrous outcome is inevitable. The church is filled with good people who are tired and frustrated, all because they're trying to do something they were never designed to do. It's not only difficult to live your new creation life, it's impossible to do so. Christ must live it through you.

The reason so many Christians feel defeated and dejected is because the church as a whole is in to recycling. The majority of ministry that's being done today is directed toward recycling the old nature through altar calls and rededications. The successes of our services are judged by how many people respond to the altar call.

For eight straight years I attended a men's retreat with several pastor friends of mine. It was held in a beautiful mountain setting. Who can't love the mountains? The fellowship among the attendees was always excellent. The retreat center staff were very gracious people, always willing to go the second mile to make sure we were comfortable. The men who hosted this retreat were great guys too. Their love for the Lord was unquestioned. The retreat commenced on a Thursday night and concluded after a Sunday morning service. Two services were held in the mornings and one at night. We had free time from noon until it was time for the evening service. The retreat was very well organized and executed. Believe it or not, the food was excellent too.

After attending this retreat for a few years, my pastor friends and I began to notice something. The same men would respond at the end of every service to receive ministry for the very thing they received ministry for after the last service. At the end of each service, there was an altar call for those who wanted to receive personal ministry. A swarm of men would flood to the front of the stage area. It was a sight to behold. Most of these men confessed they were believers. It was very common to hear weeping, and sometimes wailing, coming from these men who were being honest about their struggles. They were hungry for God and for the kind of life that only He can give. They wanted to be free from their bondage. But not many found this freedom. This cycle would repeat itself at the next men's retreat.

This is not something that just happens at men's retreats. It takes place in our church services every week. It's nothing more than a recycling of the old nature. This is precisely why the community of faith is filled with so many frustrated, defeated, and depressed believers. Many have lost all hope of ever being free. "Whom Jesus has set free is free indeed," is nothing more than a religious cliché to these individuals.

We've made living the victorious Christian life rise or fall on rededication. The church may focus on rededication, but God's focus is on eradication. Our old natures have been crucified, eradicated on the cross. We need to stop recycling it like it's still alive through rededication.

Our Old Natures' Death

"Knowing this, that our old man (our old sinful nature) was crucified with Him (Jesus), that the body of sin might be done away with, that we should no longer be slaves to sin" (Romans 6:6 NKJV). The cross was not only a tool for punishment; it was an instrument of death. When Christ died on the cross, our old sinful natures died with Him. The very next verse says, "For he who has died has been freed from sin" (Romans 6:7 NKJV). When we died with Christ, we were set free from the power of sin. Sin didn't die; we died to sin. Sin no longer has dominion over us (Romans 6:14 NKJV). Why keep rededicating something that doesn't exist anymore? We need to give the old person we were—our old natures—a decent burial and get on with living!

"Likewise you also, reckon yourselves dead indeed to sin, but alive to God in Christ Jesus our Lord" (Romans 6:11 NKJV). This verse tells us that there are two things we need to consider, that we need to reckon. We need to consider that as new creations we are dead to sin, and we're alive in Christ. Our old sinful natures were crucified with Christ on the cross; those individuals don't exist anymore. Our new lives are in the resurrected Christ. We died with Christ. We were raised with Christ. "Therefore we were buried with Him through baptism into death, that just as Christ was raised from the dead by the glory of the Father, even so we also should walk in newness of life. For if we have been united together in the likeness of His death, certainly we also shall be in the likeness of His resurrection" (Romans 6:4–5 NKJV). When we had our born-from-above experiences, we were not left with two natures battling for dominance in our lives. Our old natures were exchanged for new ones. We can't rededicate something that no longer exists.

For almost thirty years I would close our worship services with an invitation for people to come to the altar for a time of ministry. The first priorities were those who needed to accept Christ as their Lord and Savior. Evangelism was our number-one priority. Next we would turn our attention to those who needed prayer or personal ministry. Then we would make an appeal to those who wanted to join the church. And then we would begin our recycling ministry by extending the invitation to those who felt they needed to come and rededicate their lives to the Lord. Most of those who accepted this part of the invitation became repeating rededicaters. Rededication has become the churches' answer to a believer's struggle with sin. We lead them in a prayer of rededication, and then they are given a list of disciplines to follow so they can stay in fellowship with the Lord. If they fall out of fellowship with the Lord, they must repeat the process. It never crosses our minds that what they're battling with is an identity issue. If we see ourselves as sinners saved by grace, rededication will be our answer to overcoming sin and living a victorious life.

In our staff meetings we would talk about how successful the services were by how many people attended Sunday school and by how many people responded to the invitation. I know now what I didn't know then. Many people came rededicating a life that had never been dedicated, or they had no idea who Christ made them to be. They have identity issues. The only thing I was doing was helping them recycle their old natures.

Our New Natures' Birth

I have some good news for you. The good news is not that Christ lived and died but that Jesus died and now lives. We are forgiven by His death, His crucifixion. We are saved by His life, His resurrection. "For if when we were enemies we were *reconciled* (exchanged) to God through the death of His Son, much more, having been *reconciled* (exchanged), we shall be saved by His life" (Romans 5:10 NKJV; emphasis added). As a child of God, we have the resurrected life of Christ dwelling within us (Romans 8:11 NKJV). Christ died for us, so He can live His life in us and through us, as us. Remember, God will not give you anything that you can do without Him. You can't live the requirements of the old covenant. If you could, you would have to be God. You can't live the life of grace either. If you could, you wouldn't need God.

Since Jesus has become our everything, it means He's now our altar. This is why we invite people to come to Jesus, not to an altar in some building. "I beseech you therefore, brethren, by the mercies of God, that you *present your bodies a living sacrifice,* holy, acceptable to God, which is your reasonable service" (Romans 12:1 NKJV; emphasis added). The scripture says that we are to present ourselves to God as living sacrifices. An altar is not mentioned in this verse because an altar is for dead sacrifices. Jesus, the perfect Lamb of God (John 1:29 NKJV), sacrificed Himself on the cross so that our sins would be taken away, not covered. We now present ourselves to Him as a living sacrifice. We don't die on an altar so that Jesus Christ can live in us. Jesus died on a cross so we can live in Him.

A couple moved from the other side of our state to our town and began attending our church. They seemed to be a sweet couple. We bonded fairly quickly because of our geographical roots. The towns we were born and raised in were separated by only a few miles. We always thought that was interesting. One Sunday after the service this couple and I were engaged in small talk. The casual conversation we were having began to escalate slowly into an interrogation. Familiarity had bred contempt. "Why don't you give an invitation for people to come to the altar to accept Christ? "We never hear you invite people to the altar for ministry or for prayer. Why don't you give an invitation for people to come and rededicate their lives?" I don't think this couple was being insolent or discourteous toward me by their questions. They wanted answers.

Every Sunday I do what this couple accused me of not doing. The way I do it is not what they're accustomed to. At the end of every service I give people the opportunity to accept Christ as their personal Lord and Savior. That has been and remains to be a priority. An invitation for ministry is extended to everyone. The appeal I give goes something like this: "Our service may be ending today, but the ministry we offer to you never ends. I will remain here, along with our ministry team, to help you connect with Christ, to pray for you, and to minister to you in any way that we can. We'll stay here as long as we're needed." During our services on the following Sunday, we celebrate with the church family the decisions that were made during that ministry time.

Because we didn't sing fourteen stanzas of a particular hymn of invitation or invite people to an altar to rededicate their lives, we were accused of not doing what we were actually doing. The altar for offering dead sacrifices has been replaced by Jesus Christ. Jesus is now our altar. He's our lives.

Before we accepted Christ's invitation to life, we were already dead. "And you *He made alive, who were dead* in trespasses and sin" (Ephesians 2:1 NKJV; emphasis added). Verse 5 says, "Even when *we were dead* in trespasses, *made us alive* together with Christ (by grace you have been saved)" (Ephesians 2:5 NKJV; emphasis added). What does a dead person need, forgiveness or life? We don't come to Christ and die so we can live. We come to Him because we're dead so we can live! This is the exchanged life, God's quid pro quo. We give Him our old, dead natures, and a divine exchange takes place. He gives us new natures, which are His life.

When we recycle the old nature by rededication, we're in essence saying, "In order to live a godly life, we must die, again." Paul did say in 1 Corinthians 15, "I die daily" (1 Corinthians 15:21 NKJV). If Paul died daily, shouldn't we? Paul wasn't talking about rededicating his life to the Lord when he said, "I die daily." Paul's life was threatened every day because he preached the good news of Jesus Christ. In his second letter to the Corinthians, Paul said, "From the Jews five times I received forty stripes minus one. Three times I was beaten with rods; once I was stoned, three times I was shipwrecked; a night and a day I have been in the deep" (2 Corinthians 11:24–25 NKJV). Every day Paul ran the risk of losing his life because of what he did, and he came close on several occasions.

How do we deal with what Jesus said about cross-bearing? The cross is certainly an instrument of death. "Then Jesus said to his disciples, 'If any of you wants to be my follower, you must turn from your selfish ways, *take up your cross*, and *follow Me*'" (Matthew 16:24 NLT; emphasis added). Here's Luke's account of what Jesus said: "Then He (Jesus) said to them all, 'If anyone desires to come after Me, *let him deny himself,* and *take up his cross daily,* and *follow Me*'" (Luke 9:23 NKJV; emphasis added).

If Jesus says that we have to crucify ourselves on a daily basis, then so be it. Case closed. There are a couple of things I would like to bring to your attention about what Jesus said about cross-bearing. Luke quotes Jesus as saying that we must take up our crosses daily to follow Him. The word "daily" is not in Matthew's account of this same event. Theologians disagree whether or not the word "daily" should appear in Luke's account. Some say it should be in the text; others say it should not be in the text. I'll leave that debate to the experts. Whether or not "daily" is in Luke's text doesn't change what Jesus said one iota.

Taking up our crosses and following Jesus is in both texts. If you're following someone, you're going where that person is going, and you'll end up where they end up. Where was Jesus going? His destination was the cross. How many times did He go to the cross? How many times did Jesus die? If we get the answer to those two questions right, we'll begin to have a better understanding of our identities as believers. We'll begin to enjoy who we are as new creations in Christ and not get trapped in recycling the old so we can enjoy the new. There's nothing to rededicate. Our old natures were crucified with Christ on the cross. "Therefore, if anyone is in Christ, he is a new creation; old things have passed away; behold, all things have become new" (2 Corinthians 5:17 NKJV). Old things have passed away, including the old you. All things are made new, and that includes you. If it were possible for the old nature to live again, Christ would have to go back to the cross.

"For it is impossible that the blood of bulls and goats could take away sins" (Hebrews 10:4 NKJV). "But this Man (Jesus), after He had offered *one sacrifice for sins forever,* sat down at the right hand of God" (Hebrews 10:12 NKJV; emphasis added). Jesus was the perfect Lamb of God. His blood had the power do what the blood of animals could not do, take away our sins. Our sins of the past, present, and future were taken away by the blood of Christ.

What did Paul mean when he said, "Likewise you also, *reckon yourselves to be dead* indeed to sin, but alive to God in Christ Jesus our Lord" (Romans 6:11 NKJV; emphasis added)? The word "reckon" means to come to a conclusion about something after deep consideration. Let's keep the word "reckoning" in its context. Twice in Romans 6 Paul says, "knowing this": *Knowing this, that our old man was crucified* with Him (Jesus), that the body of sin might be done away with, that we should no longer be slaves to sin" (Romans 6:6 NKJV; emphasis added). In verse 9, Paul writes, "*Knowing that Christ, having been raised from the dead, dies no more*. Death no longer has dominion over Him" (Romans 6:9 NKJV; emphasis added). It's difficult to reckon something you don't know. To know means to have absolute, settled knowledge about something. Once we are absolutely convinced our old natures were crucified with Christ and our new natures were raised with Him, then we can reckon ourselves to be dead. Dying daily is not rededicating ourselves over and over again. It's acknowledging that we have died and that Christ is living His life through us, as us. What a difference this will make in our characters and in our conduct.

Before we accepted Christ as our Lord and Savior, we were dead in our trespasses and sins (Ephesians 2:1, 5 NKJV). When we accepted the Lord's invitation to life, we got exactly what a dead person needs, life. We're able to live because Jesus was willing to die. Our lives come from His death and resurrection. We live because He lives. "But this Man (Jesus), after He had offered *one sacrifice* (Himself) *forever*, sat down at the right hand of God" (Hebrews 10:12 NKJV; emphasis added). As our High Priest, Jesus could do what the other priests could not do, He sat down. The priests could never sit down because their jobs were never finished: "And *every priest stands* ministering daily and *offering repeatedly the same sacrifices*, which *can never take away sins*" (Hebrews 10:11 NKJV; emphasis added). "But *this Man* (Jesus), after He had offered *one sacrifice for sin forever, sat down* at the right hand of God" (Hebrews 10:12 NKJV; emphasis added). His job is finished. He will never have to repeat it again.

The Galatians 2:20 Life Principle

"*I have been crucified with Christ*; it is *no longer I who live*, but *Christ lives in me*; and *the life which I now live* in the flesh I live by faith in the

Son of God, who loved me and gave Himself for me" (Galatians 2:20 NKJV; emphasis added). Our old lives were crucified with Christ, and the life we're living now is Christ living His life in us. Christ is not only the source of our new lives, He's the sustainer of our new lives. He is our lives (Colossians 3:4). This new life we're living is being expressed through our same old dirt suits that we call our bodies.

What Paul says in this verse is not only eye-opening, it's very intriguing. He says that he had been crucified with Christ, past tense, and that he is no longer alive. In the same breath he says that Christ is now living in him, present tense, and that he's very much alive. He was dead; he's now alive. Paul identifies his old nature with Christ's crucifixion. He identifies his new nature with Christ's resurrection. Paul has gone from a self-centered life to a Christ-centered life. This reverses what happened in the garden of Eden, when Adam disobeyed God. Adam's rebellion took him from being spirit-conscious to being self-conscious (Genesis 3:1–7 NKJV). The last Adam, Jesus, took us from being self-conscious back to being spirit-conscious.

Before we're able to enjoy fully our birthright privileges as new creations in Christ, we must reckon that the old nature is dead. Once we have that truth absolutely settled in our spirits, we can do what we have been born from above to do, rule and reign in this life (Romans 5:17 NKJV). Our old natures are in union with death and inseparable. Our new natures are in union with Christ and is inextricable.

"Either way, Christ's love controls us. Since *we believe that Christ died for all,* we also believe that *we have all died to our old life*" (2 Corinthians 5:14 NLT; emphasis added). Paul wrote these words to the believers who were living in Corinth. As a child of God, your old life is dead. You are not a sinner saved by grace. That would be a mixture, and we know how God feels about mixture. He's not going to do something He condemns by mixing our old natures with our new natures. We are saints who sometime sin. When we take steps of stupid, we are acting in a way that is contrary to our true natures.

Knowing who we are in Christ will not make us sinless, but I'm convinced we will sin less.

Before Christ made us alive, we were dead in our sins. Does a dead person need forgiveness, or does someone who's dead need life? Forgiveness is a part of the life package, but the new lives we now have in Christ are about living as more than conquerors, no matter what the world may throw at us. This is what the exchanged life is all about. God took your old nature, and in exchange, He gave you a new nature. Death for life, this is God's quid pro quo.

"So now there is no condemnation for those who belong to Christ Jesus" (Romans 8:1 NLT). You can't say *now* without it being *now*. This scripture says it all.

AFTERWORD

It became Another

One day God spoke to Jeremiah and told him to go down to the potter's shop because He had something to teach him. Jeremiah did as he was told. He found the potter working with a piece of clay on the potter's wheel. The potter was making something, but Jeremiah couldn't tell what it was. In the process, the clay became marred, disfigured. Instead of throwing the clay away and stating over with a new batch, the potter kept his hands on the clay and began to form it again. The potter formed it into another vessel that was pleasing to him. The new vessel was inside the body of the old clay. It became another (Jeremiah 18:1–4 NKJV).

What the potter did with the clay is exactly what God did with you. He took the old you, marred and distorted by sin, and exchanged it for a new you. *It became another.* You're not a cleaned-up version of the old person. You're a completely new creation. Your spiritual DNA has been exchanged. When you had your born-from-above experience, the old you (it) was exchanged for a new you (another). You became another.

The new you still lives in the same old body. People who know you may continue to recognize you as *it* for a while. As the spiritual transformation that took place on the inside you begins to express itself through the way you live, they will begin to see that you're really not the same person. The old you was exchanged for a completely new you. This is what happened when you received Jesus as your Lord and Savior. This is what the exchanged life is all about.

Water became Another

The first miracle that Jesus performed took place at a wedding celebration. He turned water into wine. I think the significance of this being His first miracle may be overlooked. Does this miracle give us a glimpse into the purpose for His coming? Jesus didn't take poor wine and exchange it for a better wine. He took water and exchanged it for something completely different. You don't make wine out of water.

The wedding celebration was facing a dilemma. The party was about to come to a screaming halt because they ran out of wine. Mary went to Jesus and told Him about the situation and then told the servants to do whatever He told them to do. There were six stone water pots within arms' reach. It appears they were empty because Jesus told the servants to fill them with water. Each pot held twenty to thirty gallons.

We are told that these water pots were for ceremonial washings. It's interesting that they were empty. Here are a few observation snapshots worth noting. Six is the number for man. The pots were made of stone. The law was written on stone. The pots were empty. Religion does not have the ability to cleanse a person from sin or to transform them into a new creation. Religion may make a person look good on the outside, but it has no effect whatsoever on the inside of a person. Religion is man pursuing acceptance from God by doing. It will always leave a person empty, just like the pots.

Jesus told the servants to draw some out and take it to the host of the party. When he tasted the wine, his comment was, *"You have kept the good wine until now"* (John 2:10 NKJV; emphasis added). The water had become wine. *It had become another.* The new wine was in the same old stone pots. The water that was made wine had not gone through a fermenting process. Since there was no process, the wine had no beginning. That meant it had no past. It's a miracle.

What happened to the water happened to you. When you accepted Christ as your Lord and Savior, the old you became a completely new creation. It's a miracle. Like the new vessel created by the potter, like the best wine, the new you still lives in the same old body of clay.

You Became Another

"Therefore, if *anyone is in Christ*, he is a *new creation*, old things have passed away; behold, all things have become new" (2 Corinthians 5:17 NKJV; emphasis added). The Master Potter has transformed you into a new creation. The moment you said yes to Jesus, your old life ended, and your new life began. Even though you still make your home in the same old body and live in the same old neighborhood, there's a new tenant living on the inside.

Our physical bodies are what legitimize our presence here on the earth. They keep us anchored to the natural realms. The day is coming when we'll receive new bodies, which have already been procured (1 Corinthians 15:50–54 NKJV). That exchange will become a reality someday. Until then, we'll remain in our old earth suits. Even though we recognize each other by our physical appearances, the outside does not depict our true identities. The real person is on the inside.

God Brought Us Out to Take Us In

Old things, which include our old lives, have passed away. All things have become new. We have been given new lives. Salvation is about God bringing us out of the old and taking us in to the new. God never brings us out just to get us out. The purpose for bringing us out of something is to take us into something else. God brought His people out of the land of Egypt to take them into the land of Canaan (Deuteronomy 11:8–12 NKJV). Egypt is often used to describe the old life, the life of sin. The Promised Land is sometimes used to describe our new lives, what we possess as believers. This story is a beautiful analogy of what God did for us in Christ. He brought us out of our old lives of sin and took us into our new lives in Christ.

God didn't bring the Israelites out of Egypt just to get them out. That in itself would've been awesome. God had something better in mind for His people, a new life. Herein lies the danger. As children of God, we know what He's brought us out of, but we don't know what He's brought us into. The results of this ignorance is to live our lives *between* the old and the new. Most believers are trying to live victorious lives by living between their old lives and their new lives. The old life was governed by the law. The new life is governed by grace. Living in between is mixing the two. Attempting to live life between what we were and who we are is a recipe for certain failure.

Fleshing Out Our Spiritual Life Exchange: God's Quid Pro Quo

Most parents encourage their children to pursue their dreams. We tell them, "You can do whatever you set your mind to do." To "set your mind" means you start making an effort to do something. It's an expression of determination; you're focused on obtaining something. Ben Franklin said, "You can do anything you set your mind to."

As a child of God, you can set your mind on things of the flesh: "Those who live according to the flesh *set their minds on the things of the flesh*" (Romans 8:5 NKJV; emphasis added). As a new creation, you're in the Spirit, so you cannot go back and live in the flesh. But you can set your mind on the flesh. If this is the choice we make, we will act in ways that are contrary to our natures. It will be impossible for us to enjoy the benefits of our birthrights. We'll not be exempt from the consequences of our choices either.

As a child of God, you can set your mind on things of the Spirit. "*But those who live* (who set their minds) *according to the Spirit,* (will live according to) *the things of the Spirit*" (Romans 8:5 NKJV; emphasis added). When we set our minds on the things of the Spirit, we will live lives that are consistent with our natures. Our characters and conduct will be in lockstep with the Word of God. "But *you are not in the flesh but in the Spirit,* if indeed the Spirit of God dwells in you" (Romans 8:9 NKJV; emphasis added).

"*Set your mind* on things above, not on things on the earth" (Colossians 3:2 NKJV; emphasis added). We can choose to set our thoughts on things above, which is new-creation thinking, or we can choose to set our thoughts on things below, which is old-creation thinking. Victory or defeat is determined by one's thought life. How a person is living will tell you what they're thinking. What we think about determines how we live our daily lives.

To set your mind on things above means you're determined to live out your new nature. You're focused on who you are and what you have in Christ. That's what it means to walk in the Spirit. "*I say then: Walk in the Spirit, and you shall not fulfill the lust of the flesh*" (Galatians 5:16 NKJV; emphasis added). Walking in the Spirit is not some glow-in-the-dark, unattainable spiritual dimension. It's simply being determined to live our daily lives in accordance with the Word of God.

Here are a couple of simple illustrations on how to walk in the Spirit. The Word of God tells us not to lie to each other (Colossians 3:9 NKJV). How do we walk this out in our daily lives? How about this? Don't lie to each other. The Word admonishes us to forgive others as our Father has forgiven us (Ephesians 4:32 NKJV). How do we walk this out? Here's a novel idea. How about forgiving each other. Living a life that's in concert with one's new nature is simply doing what the Word instructs us to do. Walking in the Spirit is not about feelings; it's about obedience.

It all begins with a godly mindset, a determination to live our daily lives out of our new creation identities. This is possible. When we accepted and received Christ as our Lord and Savior, the Holy Spirit moved in and took up permanent residence in us. The Holy Spirit is the one who empowers and enables us to walk out our new identities as new creations. This is the exchanged life, God's quid pro quo.

Printed in the United States
by Baker & Taylor Publisher Services